TAXPAYER TEA

BY
SHARON COOPER
AND CHUCK ASAY

INTRODUCTION BY
NEWT GINGRICH

TAXPAYERS'
Tea Party
How to Become
Politically Active—
and Why

★

BY

SHARON COOPER
AND CHUCK ASAY

TAXPAYERS' TEA PARTY:
How to Become Politically Active—and Why

A Baen Book Original

Baen Publishing Enterprises
P.O. Box 1403
Riverdale, NY 10471
www.baen.com

ISBN 13: 978-1-4391-3363-7

Cover designed by Carol Russo.
Frontispiece and all interior cartoons by Chuck Asay.

First Baen printing, July 2010.

Distributed by Simon & Schuster
1230 Avenue of the Americas
New York, NY 10020

Library of Congress Cataloging-in-Publication Data

Cooper, Sharon.
  Taxpayers' Tea Party : How to Become Politically Active—and Why / by
Sharon Cooper and Chuck Asay.
      p. cm.
  Includes bibliographical references and index.
  ISBN 978-1-4391-3363-7 (trade pb : alk. paper)
  1. Taxpayers' Tea Party--Handbooks, manuals, etc. 2. Government,
Resistance to--United States--Handbooks, manuals, etc. 3. Protest move-
ments--United States--Handbooks, manuals, etc. 4. Political participation-
-United States--Handbooks, manuals, etc. I. Asay, Chuck. II. Title.
  JK1764.C549 2010
  322.4'40973--dc22
                              2010005658

Printed in the United States of America

10   9   8   7   6   5   4   3   2   1

TAXPAYERS'
Tea Party
How to Become
Politically Active—
and Why

★

CONTENTS

Introduction
to the Second Edition by
Newt Gingrich,
Former Speaker of
the U.S. House of Representatives

★ ★ ★

The story of *Taxpayers' Tea Party* is the story of American citizens stopping liberalism in its tracks and turning America in a better direction through citizen activism.

In 1993 liberals were raising taxes, creating bigger government in Washington and trying to pass a government run health system. Sharon Cooper was a local volunteer in Cobb County who was so angry and so frightened by the liberal program for a government takeover of healthcare that she was threatening to move to Costa Rica with her husband, Dr. Tom Cooper.

As a good citizen she came to see her Congressman and I urged her to defeat what was going on in Washington.

I said we need citizens like her to get actively involved and help other citizens turn their fear and anger into effective action against big government liberalism.

She enthusiastically committed herself to a life of political action and involvement. She rapidly became a leader around whom other angry and frightened citizens became involved.

The Clinton Administration had passed the largest tax increase in American history. Most hard working Americans were enraged at the reversal of the Reagan Policy of cutting taxes. The Bush tax increase of 1990 had already angered conservatives. Now the massively bigger Clinton tax increase was the last straw.

Someone had to rally taxpayers to defend their right to minimum taxation and maximum take home pay.

Activists like Grover Norquist (whose Americans for Tax Reform remains the most consistent anti-tax increase organization in America) and Rush Limbaugh (who in 1994 was already the most popular radio talk show host in America) were committed to articulating the fight against bigger government and higher taxes.

Sharon agreed to write a book about the original Boston Tea Party and the concept of a new tea party movement.

We had a lot of fun with her book during 1994 including going to Boston and having media events around the site of the original tea party.

Sharon grew from a citizen activist into a candidate and then into a successful seven term state legislator where she still serves in the Georgia House and has been chair of the Republican Caucus, one of the highest positions in the House. She is now chairman of the important Health and Human Services Committee.

With Sharon's help the movement that became the Contract with America was launched in early 1994.

With her help we elected the first Republican majority in 40 years.

With her help we turned around the big government tide and passed the first tax cut in 16 years.

With her courageous activism we kept spending under control at 2.9% a year (including entitlements) for the four years I was Speaker and balanced the federal budget for four consecutive years while paying off $405 billion in federal debt.

Courage matters.

Hard work and intelligence matters.

Sharon Cooper has all three.

Her book *Taxpayers' Tea Party* is once again needed and the citizen activism it represents is once again vital to getting America on the right track.

I hope every tea party activist in America will take the time to read Sharon's book and share its insights with their fellow citizens.

Together we can once again defeat the forces of big government and high taxes and get America on the right track to jobs, prosperity safety and freedom

The Sharon Coopers of the world are the key to that turnaround.

—Newt Gingrich

1994 Introduction by
Rush Limbaugh
—————★★★—————

The Boston Tea Party was a proud moment in American history, as everybody learned in high school. Unless, of course, you are under thirty—in which case you probably never learned the significance of the phrase, "No taxation without representation." In fact, odds are you didn't learn about King George. (You might not have heard of Boston.) Why? Because none of your sensitive multicultural-oriented teachers would dare instruct young skulls full of mush about the Tea Party . . . all those white males dressed up as Injuns, you know

Besides, as the joke goes, if taxation *without* representation was so bad, how do you like taxation *with* representation? Representation implies some sort of accountability on the part of the representatives. Those in Congress—which I have often called the most corrupt institution in America—now consider themselves accountable to no one, but the Democratic Leadership. That's what 40 years of Democratic rule will do, folks.

In *Taxpayers' Tea Party*, author Sharon Cooper, with Chuck Asay's visual assistance, makes clear that nothing about this situation is chiseled in granite. You, the voter, the American citizen, can do something about the ever-growing burden of taxation, government intrusion, and that paragon of fairness and compassion known as the federal bureaucracy. This book illustrates, in words and cartoons, that it is possible to begin to bring about a rebirth of accountability on the part of our legislators—a novel concept to them, I assure you. If you choose, you can even add a new job title to their resumes:

ex-legislator. And you may want to start with those who voted for President Clinton's record-setting tax increase—the one he enacted after campaigning on the promise of a middle-class tax cut. Well, you already know about Bill Clinton's promises.

But President Clinton is not unique in that respect. Many politicians campaign conservative and then, once safely ensconced in Washington, proceed to vote liberal. In fact, let me point to my Undeniable Truth of Life Number 23: "The only way liberals win national elections is by pretending they're not liberals." Why is that? Because: "Evidence refutes liberalism." Undeniable Truth of Life Number 4.

Taxpayers' Tea Party tells the story of the American people finally starting to take a close look at the way Congress really works—and thereupon deciding in sovereign electoral majesty to THROW THE RASCALS OUT. Why? Because without this permanent ruling class—one of the most harmful components of our political system—the will of the people would no longer be thwarted. And without the confiscatory taxes required by the modern welfare state, a huge chunk of the national economy would be unshackled. But what does Tom Foley do when the voters of Washington state vote for term limits? He sues them!

But the tide cannot be held back forever. You see, despite all the incumbency protection scams, when congressional Push comes to electoral Shove, our representatives are still answerable to the tax-paying voters—that's you and me—even if they fantasize otherwise. Sharon Cooper shows you how to get through to your Senators and Congressman by mail, phone, fax, radio interview, and street talk, and also how to make sure that when they are up for re-election, they can be held accountable.

Say, for example, that the Hon. Tax N. Spend ran on a no-new-taxes platform and you voted for him (or her)—and were outraged when he (or she) became one of the Democrat majority-of-one who in 1993 voted for the largest tax increase in American history. *Taxpayers' Tea Party* shows you how to find him (or her) and how to give him (or her) a good soaking in Boston Bay. Metaphorically, of course. (A little literary lingo there.) You will also find out just who voted against the budget, but then voted down Penny-Kasich, the bill that would have forced the Clinton Administration to honor its "New Democrat" promises. (My Undeniable Truth of Life Number 5: "There is no such thing as a New Democrat.")

If, on the other hand, you are fortunate enough to have a representative in Congress possessed of a keen mind and solid ethics, one who was not taken in by the President's "contributions" bill—no doubt because he or she listens to me—this book will tell you how to support that clear-sighted intelligent individual. You can make an effort to ensure that he or she goes back to Washington to keep the tax-and-spend crowd from reaching their hands into your back pockets.

But there's a lighter side to this book. I always advise my listeners to be of good cheer as I shine the light of truth on liberals. *Taxpayers' Tea Party* will not only inform you—it will also give you some laughs, as cartoonist Chuck Asay deftly skewers the billion-dollar absurdities of the Capitol Hill Crowd.

Taxpayers' Tea Party is for everyone worried about the ominous growth of government spending. Learn it, love it, live it. It deserves a spot on the bestseller list—right under my own best-selling tomes, of course.

But wait. Lest you conclude that this analysis is too uncritical, let me end with an objection: like my daily television and radio programs, this book is too short.

—Rush Limbaugh
February 18, 1994

12

13

17

18

22

25

HEALTH CARE

HEALTH CARE

HEALTH CARE

HEALTH CARE

HEALTH CARE

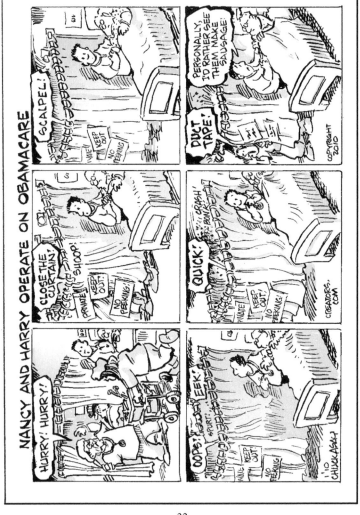

HEALTH CARE

HEALTH CARE

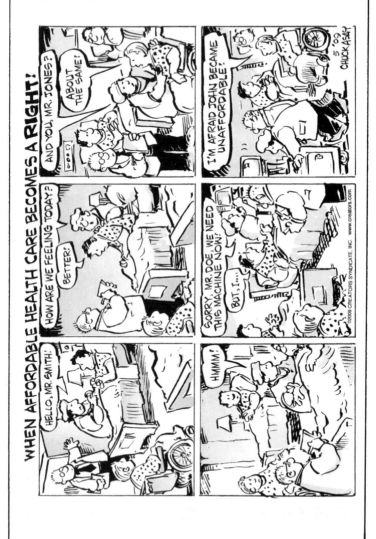

HEALTH CARE

HEALTH CARE

HEALTH CARE

HEALTH CARE

I REMEMBER WHEN I WAS VERY SICK AND YOU TOOK CARE OF ME!

I THOUGHT YOU LIKED ME!

SOCIAL CONCERNS PARKING

FOOD STAMP OFFICE
GOV'T. SHELTER
PUBLIC HEALTH CENTER

I REMEMBER THE TIME I GOT KICKED OUT OF MY HOUSE AND YOU GAVE ME A PLACE TO STAY!

MAY
COLORADO SPRINGS
GAZETTE TELEGRAPH

I REMEMBER I USED TO GET HUNGRY AND YOU WOULD GIVE ME SOMETHING TO EAT!

THEN YOU BECAME AN ACTIVIST AND GOT THE GOVERNMENT TO DO ALL OF THAT!

©1994 CREATORS SYNDICATE, INC.

ENVIRONMENT

ENVIRONMENT

ENVIRONMENT

ENVIRONMENT

ENVIRONMENT

ENVIRONMENT

ENVIRONMENT

45

ENVIRONMENT

ENVIRONMENT

WHICH ENDANGERED SPECIES DO YOU THINK THE SIERRA CLUB IS MOST INTERESTED IN PROTECTING?

...THE PREBLE'S MEADOW JUMPING MOUSE?

...THE DEMOCRATIC SENATE?

...THE GREENBACK CUTTHROAT TROUT?

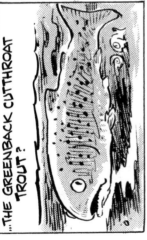

...THE MEXICAN SPOTTED OWL?

ASAY@GAZETTE.com

10'02

© 2003 CREATORS SYNDICATE, INC.

47

EDUCATION

EDUCATION

EDUCATION

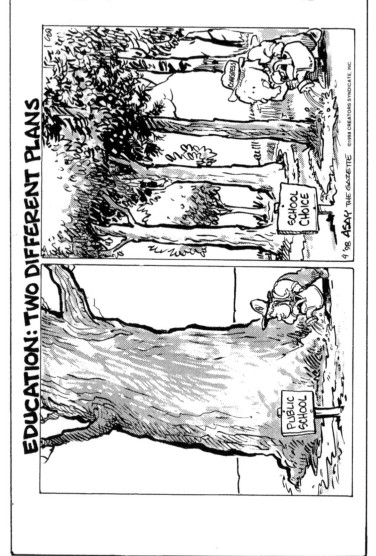

EDUCATION: TWO DIFFERENT PLANS

EDUCATION

51

EDUCATION

EDUCATION

EDUCATION

EDUCATION

SOMEDAY, PERHAPS, IN THE NOT-TOO-DISTANT FUTURE...

...IT WILL TAKE A VILLAGE TO DISCIPLINE A CHILD!

LEGAL COUNSEL

ASAY 11-'96
COLORADO SPRINGS
GAZETTE TELEGRAPH ©1996 CREATORS SYNDICATE, INC.

56

EDUCATION

RECESS

SOON, IT'LL BE...

HA! BACK IN MY DAY, WE USED TO PLAY TAG AND EVEN DODGE BALL!

IT USED TO BE...

HA! BACK IN MY DAY, WE USED TO WALK TWO MILES TO SCHOOL AND PLAY MUMBLETYPEG WITH JACKKNIVES!

©2006 CREATORS SYNDICATE, INC.

EDUCATION

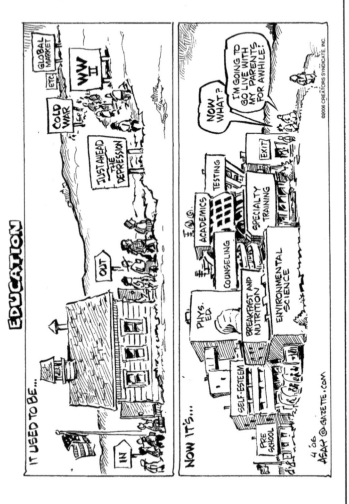

GUNS

THEY WERE ALIENS FROM ANOTHER LAND!

...AND SO WE JOIN THEIR CELEBRATION!

BOY! THINGS SURE WERE DIFFERENT BACK THEN, HUH, GRAMPS!

ASAY COLORADO SPRINGS GAZETTE TELEGRAPH

©1996 CREATORS SYNDICATE, INC. 11-96

EVEN THOUGH THEY DIDN'T SPEAK THE "RIGHT" LANGUAGE, THEY RECEIVED AID FROM EMPATHETIC NATIVES!

ON TOP OF THAT, THEY WERE RELIGIOUS FANATICS WITH GUNS!

GUNS

GUNS

GUNS

GUNS

MEDIA

MEDIA

MEDIA

MEDIA

MEDIA

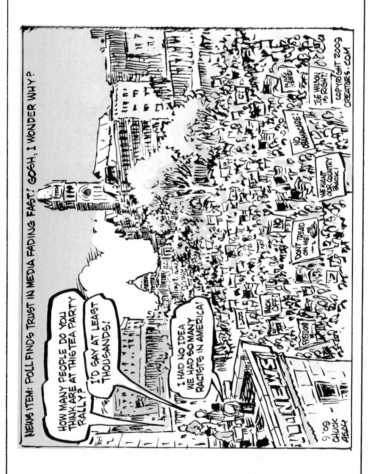

BIG GOV'T.

BIG GOV'T.

BIG GOV'T.

BIG GOV'T.

BIG GOV'T.

CAN YOU GIVE US ONE GOOD REASON WHY WE SHOULD VOTE TO CONFIRM YOU AGAIN AS THE FEDERAL RESERVE CHAIRMAN?

PAR-TEE! PAR-TEE!

MR. BERNANKE, YOUR POLICIES HAVE CONTRIBUTED TO THE HOUSING DEBACLE AND TO THE WILD EXCESSES ON WALL STREET!

GULP!

GASP!

WELL... ...FOR ONE THING, I CAN PRINT LOTS OF MONEY!

1/'10 CHUCK ASAY

BIG GOV'T.

BIG GOV'T.

BIG GOV'T.

BIG GOV'T.

DEFENSE

DEFENSE

DEFENSE

DEFENSE

MEET IRAN'S POPULARLY ELECTED PRESIDENT WHO WANTS TO WIPE ISRAEL OFF THE MAP!

HE MAKES AGREEMENTS WITH OTHER COUNTRIES, THEN BREAKS THEM TO BUY TIME TO FINISH HIS BIG ARMS PROGRAM!

HE CLOSES DOWN TROUBLE-MAKING NEWSPAPERS AND THERE IS A RELIGIOUS COMMUNITY IN HIS COUNTRY WHICH IS PERSECUTED!

DOES ANY OF THIS SOUND FAMILIAR?

©2006 CREATORS SYNDICATE, INC.

DEFENSE

DEFENSE

FINALLY...

FINALLY...

THE PARABLE OF THE MODERATE PORCUPINE

ONCE UPON A TIME, THERE WAS A PORCUPINE WHO WAS VERY, VERY SAD!

SNIFF!

"WHAT'S WRONG?" ASKED THE FOX!

"NOBODY LIKES ME," SAID MR. PORCUPINE!

"WELL, NO WONDER," REPLIED THE FOX, "YOU'RE SO PRICKLY! IF YOU WERE SOFT AND FUZZY, YOU WOULD HAVE FRIENDS!"

"GOOD IDEA," SAID MR. PORCUPINE, "I'LL TAKE CARE OF THAT NOW!"

SO MR. PORCUPINE STARTED USING QUILL SOFTENER EVERY DAY!

MOON AT THE ROAD Q.S. SOFTENER

...AND SURE ENOUGH, THE FOX CAME TO REALLY LIKE MR. PORCUPINE! HE TASTED A LITTLE LIKE CHICKEN!

ASAY 11 '98 THE GAZETTE

©1998 CREATORS SYNDICATE, INC.

87

FINALLY...

THE ROAD TO REBELLION

A Manual on How to Become Politically Active— and Why
by Sharon Cooper

"The Government is us;
we are the government, you and I."
—Theodore "Teddy" Roosevelt

Excerpts taken from the second paragraph of:

———★———

The Declaration of Independence

———★———

ACTION OF THE
SECOND CONTINENTAL CONGRESS,
July 4, 1776

We hold these truths to be self-evident, that all Men are created equal, that they are endowed by their Creator with certain unalienable Rights, that among these are Life, Liberty, and the Pursuit of Happiness—That to secure these Rights, Governments are instituted among Men, deriving their just Powers from the Consent of the Governed, that whenever any Form of Government becomes destructive of these Ends, it is the Right of the People to alter or to abolish it . . .

The Road to Rebellion, 2009

FIFTEEN YEARS AGO, when I wrote the first edition of *Taxpayers' Tea Party*, I WAS MAD AS HELL! Two elitist Yale lawyers were our country's first "Co-Presidents." Hillary, the unelected one, was on a mission to "reform" our health care system into the image of the British system. Her plan far exceeded one thousand pages and included a provision for fining a physician $10,000 and taking their license if they even helped a neighbor's sick child if that child was not one of their assigned patients. Today, as I update the book for the second edition, I'M SCARED AS HELL! We now have a president who seems to believe he has been given divine clearance to "reform" our entire health care system in the same manner. Of course, this so-called reform has nothing to do with better health care for Americans; it is all about government control. Americans need to remember <u>WHOEVER CONTROLS YOUR HEALTH CARE CONTROLS YOUR VERY LIFE!</u> Unfortunately, the U.S. Congress is under the total control of the Democrats and the leaders of both of those chambers are trying to help the President push through his liberal initiatives at warp speed. More than ever, our personal freedoms are under siege, and all Americans must act NOW in order to stop the drive to change our country into a socialist nation.

Recently I was fortunate to attend a luncheon where Herman Cain was the Keynote Speaker. Herman is an African-American gentleman who rose from humble beginnings to become the CEO of Godfather Pizza and then a candidate for the U.S. Senate. He is now an extremely successful conservative talk show host. Herman started his speech by reciting the part of the Declaration of Independence that all of us have heard over and over: "That all men are created equal, that they are *endowed by their Creator with certain unalienable Rights, that among these are Life, Liberty and the pursuit of Happiness.*"

Then he asked us if any of us knew what followed that great and familiar statement. None of us remembered, so he recited it verbatim: "That to secure these Rights, Governments are instituted among Men, deriving their just powers from the consent of the governed, That *whenever any Form of Government becomes destructive of these ends, it is the Right of the People to alter or to abolish it.*"

Our Forefathers were talking to us, everyday citizens, for we are the governed. Despite what the current radicals think, our elected officials derive whatever power they have from us, the Governed, not vice versa. The current administration's utter disdain for the American people is unbelievable! When the President and congressional leaders start calling American citizens, who are just scared and speaking out against a piece of proposed legislation, names such as stupid, evil mongers, mobsters, brown shirts, un-American, thugs and political terrorists, you know there is "Trouble in Dixie," as Southerners say.

As citizens we have two ways of altering our government; our voice and our vote. Now is the time for Americans all over this country to let their voices be heard—loud and clear. As with the first Tea Party participants so long ago in Boston, Americans are flocking to town hall meetings and 21st century Tea Parties around the country by the thousands. Change in Washington will not come overnight, and this momentum must be sustained.

November 2010 will be the time that we can right the direction of our country with our votes. If you think your one vote doesn't count, think again. Early in our country's history one lone

Congressman's vote made English our national language instead of German. Also, Clinton's 1993 tax increase passed by one lone vote in the Senate. Every vote is important.

The 2010 election is shaping up to be one of, if not the most, crucial in our Nation's history. To stop the Democrats, who hold absolute control of the White House and the Congress, we must win enough seats to totally take away their filibuster ability in the Senate a one seat margin is not enough. This will stop the Democrats' ability to cram their liberal agendas down our throats.

Are the Republicans perfect? Absolutely not! When they were in total control they moved away from their conservative values and consequently were voted out of power. Personally, I think that taught the Republicans a very valuable lesson and that they have learned from their mistakes. No matter what, they are better than the dictatorial leaders we have now!

Americans with any concern about the direction of the country must not stay away from next year's elections. Everyone must vote. If you are not registered to vote, do so now. Call your Secretary of State's office and they will either send you a voter registration form or tell you where to get one. Before each election there is a cutoff date for registering to vote, so don't wait until the last minute and think you can show up on Election Day and vote. _**Please**_ don't think that just because you registered to vote that you will be called for jury duty. Most states now use car registrations or drivers license data to compile the list for jury duty. Even if you do get called, wouldn't you want people like yourself serving on the jury if you were on trial? Also, wouldn't it be worth serving in order to help throw the current rascals in Washington out of office?

As I said before, the Republicans are certainly not perfect and they blew some golden opportunities, but at least they believe in personal freedom. So, in 2010 let's give the Republicans the victories they need to stop the radical agenda being pushed by the Democrates in congress. It is critical for Americans to remember that our country has only two major political parties. A vote for any other party no matter how well meaning will just be a vote to help the Democrats stay in office. Also in 2010 and 2012, we cannot afford to have a single, hard working, concerned taxpayer stay home or vote for anyone other than a Republican candidate.

In 1992 when I was a political novice and so angry about what was happening in my government, I found it very difficult to find out how to become involved. That is why I wrote the first edition of this book. I also needed a bit of a refresher course on just how my government really worked. I hope this new update will save you the trials and tribulations that I suffered, and make it easier for you and your friends to become politically active in a positive and successful way. I also hope that the book motivates you to involve others in the quest to take back our government.

Sharon Cooper

The Road to Rebellion, 1994

WHAT HAS HAPPENED SINCE BILL CLINTON was elected president to turn a 51-year-old housewife into a political activist? I suppose it was my growing outrage over the tax-and-spend ways of the majority of our senators and representatives in Congress. With one of their own at the other end of Pennsylvania Avenue it's been "Katie, bar the door!" since Clinton's First Day.

Now more than ever before, American taxpayers are being asked to tighten our belts while our elected officials in Washington continue to indulge in a frenzy of spending. They blithely ignore our pleas for deficit reduction and a balanced budget, while using versions of "newspeak" to try and keep us fooled. "Contribution" and "Investment" have become synonyms for "Taxes," and "Compassion" a code word for profligacy.

Of course, the current president and his quick-change artists did not invent outrageous taxation. Though it has taken Bill Clinton to bring it to full expression, my anger really began in 1986, with the first retroactive taxes in my memory. This massive tax increase killed the real estate market and put the country into one of the worst recessions ever. It also undermined my own personal economic security. My husband and I had worked hard, lived within our means and planned carefully for our future. With the stroke of a

97

pen, Congress turned our life upside down. Our fatal mistake was trusting Congress, and making investments that this august body had personally blessed with tax advantages to encourage their use.

"Put not thy faith in Princes," Machiavelli said, and it does seem that once elected, most Congressmen (and women) become petty "lords and ladies." Once in Washington they forget that they are employees, *servants* of their constituents. All of a sudden they are dealing with such vast sums of money that they cannot conceive of it as real currency. It appears to be more like Monopoly money to them! They forget, or worse simply don't realize or care, that their free spending decisions will have serious and long-lasting consequences on the people back home, the people who elected them in the first place

Apparently, these elected members of Congress have felt for many years that the seeming political apathy of the middle class is a sign that this group is deaf, dumb, blind and stupid. This year I think that millions of us from the middle class are going to prove to these soon-to-be deposed Congressmen that they have been disastrously mistaken about us. We are like a sleeping giant who is rapidly awakening, and in the process becoming filled with a terrible resolve. We may have to tolerate Clinton until 1996, but in 1994 we can change the balance of power in Congress and thereby end his ability to yet further tax and regulate us midway through his term.

America in the '80s showed the world how reduction of the tax and regulation burden can revive the economy. What the rest of the world learned, we have forgotten. In 1993, while Germany was lowering tax rates to stimulate its economy, President Clinton was fighting for another massive tax increase for the American taxpayer. This was another "soak the rich" scheme, just as George Bush predicted would happen in the fall of 1992 if Clinton had his way. "The rich" turned out to be anyone with an income of more than $35,000 a year.

Clinton has gone all-out to have his way. When a Democratic Congressman disagreed with the proposed tax increases—Senator

Shelby of Alabama—Clinton punished him by taking jobs out of his state. This was good-old-boy politics at its worst. I guess what finally pushed me over the edge was having two Georgia representatives, John Lewis and Cynthia McKinney, join 80 other Democratic members of Congress in demanding that any Democrat who did not vote for the president's budget, replete with massive tax increases, would not be allowed to continue to hold a committee chairmanship.

I thought we sent legislators to Washington to represent the people and not just to give an automatic vote of approval and their unconditional support to the Democratic leadership. This is still a constitutional republic, not a dictatorship, isn't it? I agreed with Newt Gingrich that "40 years is enough" of Democratic control of the House. It's time for us, acting individually and collectively, to make that clear.

The vote on the tax increase proved to me that one person could make a difference. The enthusiastic lobbying of members of Congress by concerned citizens from all over the country had an effect. If we had changed the vote of *just one more* senator or representative, we would have stopped that budget, with its terrible tax increase, dead in its tracks. We came so very close that year. Just wait until next time.

As angry as I had been about Clinton's tax and spend ways, I'm even more upset about the upheaval he is creating in our society. During the entire presidential campaign Clinton was continually bashing "the rich" in his speeches. To hear him tell it, anyone who made over $200,000 a year did it at the expense and to the detriment of the poor. Pitting the well off against the poor and disadvantaged causes a type of class warfare that sets black against white, professionals against blue collar worker, and makes for social unrest throughout the entire fabric of our social structure. Such tactics hark back to the very beginnings of socialism and fascism, and have been used successfully ever since; it is up to us to brand politicians who engage in such demagoguery as the cynical manipulators that they are.

Just to keep the record straight, during the 1992 campaign Hillary Rodham Clinton said she made $70,000 a year, which by her standards would not make the Clintons "rich." After the election it was disclosed that she made closer to $250,000. Such hypocrisy! Or should we call it lying?

To follow up their preparations for the most massive tax hijack in history, the Clintons set about stirring up a so-called "national health care crisis," and labeling all physicians as greedy, uncaring monsters. This rhetoric made my blood boil; I live with one of these "monsters." Since 1963 he has worked 60 to 80 hours a week taking care of patients, often at the expense of his own health. For my husband, patients have always come first.

Both Clintons [and Obama] must be students of Groucho Marx (or is it Karl), for he said that "Politics is the art of looking for trouble and finding it everywhere, diagnosing the wrong therapy and applying all the wrong remedies."

That would certainly apply to the Democrats' approach to health care. Even Senator Daniel Patrick Moynihan has finally admitted that there is no "health crisis." Yes, there are problems that need correcting, but we don't need to redesign the whole system because 15 percent (or less) of the population has a problem.

Americans had better wake up and start screaming to their Congressman and Senators. Just think for a moment—if the government controls our health care, it controls our very lives. If you want an example of what government controlled health care will be like, talk to someone who has had a loved on in a V.A. hospital. It's *not* a pretty picture. I've been there with my Dad!

Talk to someone on Medicare. Ask them what services they previously received under that plan and what the government has taken away, bit by bit, year after year. As Dr. Bernadine Healy, former director of the National Institutes of Health, has stressed, "Under a federally controlled health plan, what the government giveth, the government can taketh away."

In January of 1993 I felt so powerless that I had to do something. I dragged my husband to Washington for a meeting with Sen. Sam Nunn (a great and unselfish servant of his country, his state and his constituents) and anyone else who would listen. Perhaps this helped focus Senator Nunn. It certainly helped me. I became even more determined to become politically active! Once I returned home, I entered into an extensive networking campaign. I wrote everyone I knew, sending them articles supporting my views on taxes, this administration and Congress, and asking them to write or call their Congressman and Senators.

I talked to anyone who would listen and tried to get them to become active too. It got to the point where my family made me declare "Clinton-free" days so that we could all have a break once in a while!

My husband and I wrote to every doctor in our county, as well as to many who would vote in our old congressional district, which had a Democratic congressman. I sent copies of articles and information supporting a vote against the tax increase. We also sent each physician the address, phone numbers and fax numbers of Rep. Buddy Darden and asked them to contact him and try to change his vote to a "No" on the tax increase.

I visited and got to know Newt Gingrich, my Republican congressman and kept asking him what more I could do to change things for the better. He put me in touch with Americans for Tax Reform, a group headed by Grover Norquist. That organization was beginning to run radio ads in certain key congressional districts explaining what it would mean to voters if the Congress approved the tax increase. They needed my financial help to accomplish this task and I was glad to give it.

Up until 1992, a so-called conservative Democrat, Rep. Buddy Darden, had represented my district. A typical "Southern Conservative," he talked one way at home and voted another in Washington. Doesn't that sound like President Clinton? No wonder they get along so well! When the district was redrawn in 1991 and a Republican congressman, Rep. Newt Gingrich, took over what used to be some of Rep. Darden's area, I began to see the difference. Where Darden was ignoring the wishes of the taxpayers in his new district and was happy to be photographed jogging with Clinton, Gingrich listened to his constituents, voted again the increase and through his leadership kept all 175 Republicans together against the tax hike.

I learned that there was something I could do to make my feelings known. I contributed $1500.00, which went to help pay for radio time to convince Darden that a second vote for Clinton's tax hike would be a serious mistake. What a sense of empowerment it gave me to drive through Cobb County and hear those ads tell its citizens what Buddy Darden's tax bill would do to them. This year I will make an independent expenditure and fight a one-woman war against at least one tax-and-spend Congressman. And you can too! Details follow. Remember the legislator you choose to "take on," as we say in the South, does not have to be from the congressional district in which you live, or even be from your state.

I found out that it is true that bad politicians are elected and stay in office because good people don't participate in politics. You don't have to feel helpless. You can **DO** something now! One person **CAN** make a difference.

Barbara Jordan once said, "The stakes are too high for Government to be a spectator sport." One by one, working with a common purpose, we can change government so that it interferes with us less, spends less of our money and lowers the tax burden on its citizens. It's time for a Taxpayers' Tea Party!*

*As with any party, a Taxpayers' Tea Party is more fun with friends. Just as he did with Sally Jefferson, Grover Norquist and Americans for Tax Reform have lent us a hand by supplying us with a great many facts and figures included herein. (Any mistake we have made with them are of course our own, and none of Grover's responsibility.) Thanks, Grover and ATR!

Networking

Sharing your political view with others.

THERE SEEMS TO BE A GREAT DEAL of misinformation surrounding the political process in our country. You don't have to know somebody or be someone special to become involved. You don't have to belong to either major political party and no one is going to check your financial status. Once you believe, as Chester Bowles said, *"Government is too big and too important to be left to the politicians,"* you will have taken the first step toward becoming someone who counts in the political process.

The next step, after making the decision to get involved, is to seek out candidates on the local, state and national level that have beliefs similar to yours and whose political ideals and goals you can support. Also, you need to begin identifying politicians who should be "retired" and then begin to build your case against them.

Once you have found someone you like, tell your friends and explain why you believe in them. What makes one politician different from another is their beliefs and the strength of their determination to fight for those beliefs in the legislative arena. Therefore, one of the most useful things you can do to help a candidate is to spread their message among your friends. This is networking .

Networking, in a political sense, simply means discussing the political issues of the day with any friend or acquaintance who will listen, and who might then be convinced to support a certain candidate or specific political issue. Keep at it! Networking isn't hard, it just takes action and practice. Before November '92 I had zero political or networking experience. I am now comfortable discussing my view with anyone. All it takes is practice!

Part of that ease comes from being thoroughly familiar with the issues to be discussed, including arguments that those with opposing views might bring up. I collect articles and other types of information that can lend support to my views and have those readily available to share with others.

Who are these "others"? Folks often say to me, "I don't know many people." But just stop and think of everyone you come in contact with each week. You will be amazed at the actual number of individuals you interact with during that time.

First, list all your family members, not just brothers and sisters, but in-laws, cousins, assorted spouses and even their in-laws. Next, list all the organizations to which you belong, or with which you have some type of contact. As an example, today I spent ten minutes at the end of my garden club meeting encouraging the eighteen members present to study the President's health care proposals very carefully, because I feel that this plan will be extremely hazardous to our health.

I also gave these ladies specific examples to reinforce my views. After answering their questions, I gave each one a sheet containing the addresses, phone, fax numbers and email addresses of all our Georgia's congressmen and senators. I also gave them the web address where they could read the entire 1,016 pages of the House health bill. I encouraged each garden club member to write her legislators and to encourage their family and friends to do the same.

Each member was asked to study the issue carefully and to discuss it with everyone they knew, just as I had done with them. To me this is networking at its best—and it works! My personal networking score at that meeting: 18. If they pass the information along to others, just think how many people I have helped reach.

Don't be afraid to talk with members of your church or

synagogue, people at work (just keep extended conversations to your lunch break or free time), and anyone else who will listen. If someone doesn't agree with you, what's the worst that will happen? They may get a little annoyed. Big deal. If you're unlucky, they may want to argue but at least you will have taken an active part in the democratic process. Who knows, you may win and they could change their viewpoint.

"*A silent majority and government by the people is incompatible,*" Tom Hayden said this several years ago. While I disagree with Hayden's views on almost everything, he is absolutely right about silence. Issues need to be discussed by *all* those who are affected. To quote my husband, a retired Air Force colonel, "*Silence is not a sign of neutrality, it is a form of surrender.*" It looks like the current health care debate has awakened the sleeping giant; the American people are silent no more.

Social Networking

by Cathy And Allan Lipsett

FIFTEEN YEARS AGO, when this book was first published, there were only 3.2 million Internet users worldwide and email was in its infancy. At that time, Congressmen were wary of using email because of the lack of security and the inability to track constituent comments.

Now every Congressman has an email address (listed in the back of this book) as well as the White House and probably even the Obama's dog.

While e-mailing your Congressman, the President and other elected leaders is one of the quickest, easiest and cost-effective ways to voice your opinion, don't forget about using email in your networking. I used to advise political hopefuls to drag out their Christmas card list for the names and addresses of friends and family to contact for support. Now its even easier to pick through your Outlook address book—or hit send all—to spread the message that you wish friends, family and even business acquaintances to hear.

The term Social Media may be a term that's foreign to those of us born before the laptop era. But these websites—Facebook, MySpace, YouTube, Twitter, Blogger, Care2, Classmates, LinkedIn or Bebo—are growing at an exponential rate.

Let's look at how to use just a few of these.

Facebook: It's not just for kids anymore. With more than 70 million users, Facebook has nearly doubled in usage in the past year. You can use your "Wall" to preach the message about conservative issues or join or set up your own "Cause" fan page. The Causes Exchange on Facebook has nearly 25 million monthly users. There's an interest out there in cyberspace with your name on it.

Twitter: Do you speak in bumper stickers? Twitter allows you to send short messages of up to 140 characters to followers. You can update and comment on the foibles of your tax-and-spend Congressman or comment on what the President just said in a news conference. This is designed for cell phones—better yet, smart phones like the iPhone—so you'll need to become proficient in texting.

Blogger: If you've got something to say that requires a long form of communication, as in multiple paragraphs of reasoned logic, you can set up your own blog for free on Blogger. Other services are Typepad and WordPress. Since these are on the Internet, it's possible a search engine on one of the Google, Yahoo, or other news sites will pick up your comments.

YouTube: If you would rather say it than type it, make a video of your comments and add background music and post it on YouTube. Use a webcam or cell phone video. Check out one citizens stance against "Obamacare" at **Death Panel Alan Smithee** on You Tube

Social media allows you to network with like-minded activists and expands your reach in spreading your message.

Sample Networking Letter

Dear Friend:

I am enclosing a number of newspaper and magazine articles about the Obama Administration, which I think clearly indicate his extreme liberalism and other radical views. The articles also outline how he plans to implement these ideas into government programs via proposed legislation. These programs will have a major negative impact on all of our lives.

Please network this information to your friends and relatives all over the country. Let's touch every state! We need to stop this administration **NOW** before those in charge bankrupt the country and ruin the best health care system in the world. Stay abreast of the news . . . read everything you can on the various topics. Obama is moving fast and has plans to "reform" *everything*.

Please call, email, fax and write your Congressman and Senators. I email or fax first, then send the same information by mail, if I feel a more detailed letter will help emphasize my point. It is also helpful to thank those legislators who stand against bills you don't want to pass, even lawmakers from other states.

Your letters don't have to be long. In fact, it's better to be short, sweet and to the point. Find a nice way to let the official know that you will be watching how they vote and that you will use that information in deciding who to support in the next election. DO NOT actually threaten to support someone else.

Thank you very much for your help.
Sincerely,

Sharon Cooper
Sharon Cooper

──────★──────
Face to Face Meetings
──────★──────

SCHEDULING AN APPOINTMENT to talk with your elected officials may not be as hard as you think, especially with those representing you on the state level.

Most state legislatures meet for a very limited time each year and during that period the pace is very fast and extremely hectic. Members rush from being in the chamber, where they vote on bills, to multiple committee meetings. Georgia, for example, has a 40-day legislative session and House members serve on 4-6 committees. Some days I put my purse in my office at 8 AM and never return until I pick it up to go home at 8 or 9 PM. Scheduling a sit down meeting of any length with your representative during session becomes difficult, but not impossible, if you are flexible and do not mind driving to the state capitol.

Citizens often visit the state capitol during session to support or to attempt to stop a bill that is coming up for a vote. They stand outside the House or Senate Chamber and send in messages asking legislators to come out for a quick chat. Usually they just ask the legislator to vote yea or nay on an issue and give reasons for their position. Sometimes they will also bring written information to support their view.

Try not to be offended if a legislator does not leave the chamber to visit with you. They may need to stay on the floor to vote or they may be listening to a debate. Of course, some don't want to be lobbied because they have already decided how they are going to vote.

Since most legislatures are part time, legislators have "real" jobs back home in their district. After session or just before the next session begins is the best time to schedule a meeting for an in depth discussion on an issue. Most states do not fund district offices, but capitol office secretaries work year round and can schedule a meeting for you. Without an official district office, your representative may meet you at the local coffee shop, library, their place of work or some other public establishment.

Be sure to check when your legislature meets because it varies from state to state. California, Pennsylvania, and New York are full time legislatures and meet year round. Texas is part time and only meets every other year, but it provides district offices for its members.

U.S. Congressmen are a little harder to pin down because they represent a larger number of citizens than their state counterparts and because they work year round in Washington D.C. A U.S. House member has over 630,000 citizens in their district and the two U.S. Senators represent everyone in their state. In Georgia that means the U.S. Senators represent almost ten million men, women, and children.

Of course, members of the U.S. Congress have offices and full staffs in both Washington and their home district. Their staff members are often specialists in specific areas such as tax law, social security regulations, Veterans affairs, etc. Many citizens soon realize that they don't need to meet with their Congressman to have their problems solved or to express their views.

If you still want to meet with your Congressman or Senator, call their office way ahead of when you would like to meet. Do not take a chance on just dropping in and expect to be seen. Congressmen on the east coast usually come home each week and many have office hours on Monday morning and all day Friday. They also get frequent breaks during the year and schedule constituent visits during those times.

The further west you go, the harder it is on your representative to return home each week so they may be less available. Of course, if you are willing to go to Washington you can try to get an appointment there. A Congressman's schedule is also crazy, so you really have to be flexible. After flying to Washington from Atlanta, my first appointment with Senator Nunn was almost cancelled because he wanted to catch an earlier flight home to Georgia because it had started to snow.

The U.S. Congress does not have regularly scheduled times for members to be in either the House or Senate chambers, so the only place to try and catch members if you do not have an appointment is by visiting the legislative office buildings. At best you will get a staff member, and most likely a receptionist will just record your position on an issue since you do not have an appointment.

No matter whether you are meeting with a state representative or U.S. Congressman, time will be of the essence. Be prepared, know your facts, write down the points you want to make so you don't forget anything and always be polite. Be as concise as possible and always be truthful. It is also best if you offer positive solutions when appropriate. All elected officials respond best to constituents that are positive and those that do not just complain and whine. When a legislator does not agree with you do not get angry, curse, or threaten them. Threats are taken very seriously, and you could find yourself facing state or federal law officials. Telling the official politely that their position could influence your future support in a negative manner is not a threat.

As I have said, do not get mad—legislators have long memories. A trial lawyer called me out of the chamber one day and tried to convince me to vote for a bill he wanted. I listened politely and then told him honestly that I could not vote for that bill. At that point he started screaming at me saying I was just too stupid to understand the issue. He made me so mad, my response was, "Oh no, no, no. You're the one that's stupid because I get to go back inside and push the red button against your bill." To this day, trial lawyers are not high on my list and usually I vote against them.

Helpful Hints: Many U.S. Congressmen served in their state legislatures before running for higher office so your state representatives know many of them personally. I often relay messages for constituents to Georgia's U.S. Congressmen and you might utilize this avenue in your state as well.

Never underestimate the power of your state representatives and senators. In general, the laws they pass have much greater and more immediate impact on your day to day life than those passed by the U.S. Congress. Our jobs are just not as glamorous and draw much less press attention.

---★---

How to Write Your Congressman

---★---

🖨 To fax email or write . . . ✉
that is the question.

WHEN IT COMES TO THE FIELD OF COMMUNICATIONS, there has been an explosion of technology in the last fifteen years. It seems unbelievable, but when I wrote the first edition to *Taxpayers' Tea Party* there was absolutely no mention of email. Now email has become so prevalent that the U.S. Post Office is running into serious financial difficulties due to the drastic reduction in the amount of first class mail being sent by Americans.

Since writing a letter takes time and effort, it is still one of the most effective ways (next to face-to-face discussions) to communicate your deep concern about an issue to your legislators.

Unfortunately, reaching your Representative or Senator in Washington in a timely manner has become more difficult since some fool sent anthrax poison to numerous offices via mail. Since letters can be delayed for several days as they are waiting to be scanned, my motto has become: Fax an abbreviated version now; write a letter later if needed.

Letters from an elected official's constituents receive attention first. This is only human nature, since constituents are the only people who can vote for them. Therefore, always include your complete address on any form of correspondence to *your* Congressman.

Before you pick up the phone, put pen to paper or type on a keyboard to let your elected representatives know your thoughts, here are a few suggestions that will hopefully make the process easier and more effective. Remember that the following dos and don'ts are only guidelines, not hard and fast rules.

First, if you need to know your legislator's actual mailing address, go to the Congress.org website and type in your zip code, preferably all nine numbers. All state level and federal officials representing you should be listed, along with their contact information. Congressmen will have both a local and a Washington office and letters sent to either should reach their intended recipient. The Congress.org website tells you a lot about those serving in the House and Senate. Information such as their committee assignments, a biography, and other useful facts can be found on the website. You can request weekly emails that monitor how they vote on issues and get special news sent to you as well. This is a free service.

If you are writing, faxing or emailing a U.S. senator, the letter should be addressed to "The Honorable John Doe" and the salutation should be "Dear Senator" or "Dear Senator Doe." A letter to a U.S representative would be addressed to "The Honorable Jane Doe" and the salutation could be "Dear Representative" or "Dear Congresswoman/Congressman Doe." For clarification, the definition of a legislator is one who makes laws, especially for a political unit. (This definition fits both members of the U.S. Congress and those elected to state legislatures. In this book I have used them interchangeably. I have also referred to Congressman or used the word he instead of always trying to be politically correct and noting he/she. Just a note of interest, although women make up more than 50% of our nation's population, they are still greatly underrepresented in elected office. For example in the Georgia Legislature out of 236 seats, women hold 14% of the seats.) A salutation for a committee chairperson or the Speaker would be "Dear Chairman Doe," "Dear Chairwoman Doe" or "Dear Madam Speaker."

The main thing to remember is not to be intimidated. Your Representative or Senator works for you and they put on their pants or dresses just like you do each morning. Get busy and contact your legislator now!

The central switchbord number for Congress is 202-225-3121.

 Some Dos and Don'ts

1. If at all possible, avoid using a form letter, fax or email. It is best to compose your own correspondence and it doesn't have to be fancy or even elegant. If an issue is important enough to write about, it deserves your own words. If you must start with a form letter, at the very least, take the time to recopy it and personalize it with some of your own words. Of course, even if you don't have time to send the very best, any letter, fax or email is better than nothing.

2. Keep it simple and on a single page. Being brief is always best.

3. For "old fasioned" letters use letterhead or plain white paper. Handwritten letters are certainly acceptable and carry a lot of weight because of the thought and effort involved, but make sure your handwriting is legible.

4. Do not be sarcastic or insulting. Abusive messages are much less likely to be taken seriously. I sometimes amuse myself by writing exactly what I'd like to say first and then revising it into something much more politically and socially acceptable. "Your stupid short-sighted vote can only be excused by your notorious ignorance!" becomes "While you have already clearly listened to a select group of individuals who will benefit from your vote, perhaps you are unaware of the terrible side effects and unintended consequences that will now inevitably arise."

5. Organize your thoughts carefully. Write them down in logical order, then pretty them up. Give your reason for writing in the very first sentence of your letter, email or fax.

6. Limit the correspondence to one issue. If you find you are dealing with two or three issues, write three letters, emails or faxes, and send them at four or five day intervals.

7. Include any supporting information, dates, numbers, statistics, etc. that back up your position in your second paragraph. Occasionally, with a letter you may want to include a clipping or article to support your views. If so, refer to it in this paragraph. Underline or use a highlighter on the section in the article that contains the specific information you want to stress.

8. In the third and last paragraph you should state the action you would like your Congressman to take. If you have alternative solutions to a specific problem, be sure to include them.

9. If possible, limit your letter, email or fax to three paragraphs. If you can't, remember that the first, second and last paragraphs of any correspondence are the ones most likely to be read and relayed to the Congressman's database of voter opinion. Congressmen cannot possibly read every piece of correspondence they receive, especially on issues that generate huge public outcries. Your letter, email or fax will most likely be read by an aide assigned to that specific issue (i.e. health care, urban affairs, or gun control) and the number of pros and cons will be counted. If your letter offers a unique idea or solution it is much more likely to brought to the personal attention of the intended Congressman.

10. When closing the letter, email or fax thank the congressman for considering your request and say that you will look forward to hearing where he stands on the issue. Also mention that you will be paying attention to how he votes on the matter. Any member of Congress should realize that if

you have taken the time to express your opinion on a certain matter, that his vote on that issue might greatly influence his approval rating with you at election time.

11. Keep copies of your letters, emails and faxes and use them to inspire your friends and neighbors. Let them adapt your letter for their own.

12. It always pays to say thank you. Once your Congressman has voted in a manner favorable to your cause, drop him a note (a postcard will do) saying thank you for that action. This is the time to say something like "Your vote on this legislation will certainly have a positive bearing on my vote come Election Day."

13. Make a point of getting to know your Congressman NOW! Attend a town hall meeting or a civic club meeting where your elected official is going to speak. Be sure to introduce yourself afterwards. (A phone call to the Congressman's local office should provide you with the information as to when and where he will appear next.)

If appropriate, when you write, email or fax, your Congressman you should mention that you enjoyed hearing him speak at an event such as the January Rotary Club meeting in your town, or wherever. This type of self-introduction indicates to the Congressman that you are an active member of your community and likely to be politically responsible. A person who pays attention to issues and is lkely to vote.

WRITING OTHER LEGISLATORS

As already mentioned earlier, concentrate on your own Representatives and Senators first. But most bills do not affect only one district or one state. On the federal level they impact the lives of people across our nation. Therefore, I believe you have the right to contact and express your views to any member of the U.S. Congress. Given that almost all of us have friends and family scattered across America that we can influence. With the ease of today's communications, legislators would be wise to listen to everyone that express opinions and concerns to them.

When an issue under consideration is of national significance, try contacting every Representative and Senator who serves on a committee considering the legislation. While some bills are only assigned to a single committee, others such as the budget will be under review by numerous committees. If you have family, friends or professional contacts in a legislator's district or state, be sure to mention that fact. Even better, have those individuals contact legislator too.

If a legislator serving on one of these committees is already on your side, send a letter, fax, or email supporting them and saying thank you for their position. This is certainly a welcomed gesture. Some of the loneliest people in Washington are the anti-tax-and-spend legislators. Legislators receive both pro and con correspondence on almost every issue and a tally is almost always kept. A positive contact from you may neutralize the effect of a negative one.

Feel free to write a legislator that you consider to be in the "enemy" camp on a given issue. This person shouldn't be threatened. As always your contact should be polite with absolutely no profanity. Your letter, fax or email will notify the official of your disagreement and your displeasure. It is okay to let the legislator know that you will be in contact with friends and family who live in their area to share your views on their representative.

A legislator who is "on the fence" about an issue is where a massive letter-writing campaign may be most effective. You want to saturate this person's office with individualized letters. Please remember you are more likely to get farther with people by being nice.

Sample Letter to a Congressman

This is the first letter that I actually wrote to an elected official. Isn't it sad we are discussing the same issues today?

Senator Sam Nunn
Washington, D.C. 20510

Dear Senator Nunn:

This letter is to express my strong opposition to President Clinton's (Obama) health care plan. The American health care system is presently the finest in the world. Why else would people from all over the World come here for treatment? We have no health care crisis! Nothing is perfect, but the problems inherent in our health care coverage can be fixed without a radical overhaul of the entire system. If the President's program is so wonderful, why have all federal employees, including members of Congress, been given the choice to continue with their private insurance plan?

If implemented, the President's health care package will mean decidedly less health care (with greatly reduced quality) for most Americans. Rationing or denial of care would become an immediate reality and all of this would be at a significantly higher cost. A cost that is not being presented in a realistic, truthful manner to the American taxpayer.

When has Government managed anything more efficiently than the private sector? To prove my point, just remember that in 1965 the Government estimated that its new Medicare program would cost $9 billion annually by 1990. The correct cost for 1990 was $106 billion, quite a difference! In fact, that Government-run program has been a major culprit in the rising cost of health care. I believe that if enacted, the President's plan would bankrupt our country by 2050. Our current taxes and deficit will seem like peanuts by comparison. Where will Congress find the money to pay for such an all-inclusive package without more massive tax increases? NO MORE TAXES, THANK YOU!

More than any other factor, I abhor the loss of freedom the President's Health Plan will entail. America is supposed to still be a democracy and Americans should be able to choose their physicians and their health insurance, even if this means they choose to go without coverage.

Senator Nunn, as always, I am grateful for your responsible and independent representation of Georgians. I know you support our quest for a REASONABLE solution to assist the 15% of Americans who are without health insurance, or who are currently dissatisfied with their coverage. Please help enact a bill that allows a person to take his or her insurance from one job to another, that offers pools of insurance for high-risk patients and patients with pre-existing disease, that addresses the cost of health insurance and that enacts tort reform. The Republicans strongly support these types of changes and the Congress could act quickly in a bipartisan manner to give Americans health coverage while maintaining our free enterprise system.

Sincerely

Sharon Cooper

Sharon M. Cooper, R.N., M.S.N.

Senator Nunn's Response

United States Senate
Washington, D.C. 20510

July 29, 1993

Dear Sharon:

Thank you for contacting me with your thoughts on the Senate version of President Clinton's budget deficit reduction package. As you know, the Senate approved this legislation on June 24th by a vote of 50–49. I voted against this legislation.

After supporting the President's deficit reduction targets in March, I was disappointed that the package as reported by the Finance Committee and amended on the Senate floor failed to include sufficient spending cuts, growth incentives, or entitlement restraints. I have enclosed a copy of a speech I gave on the Senate floor, which explains my opposition to this legislation and elaborates on the steps we must take if we are serious about reducing the deficit. I will continue to push for these measures in the future.

It was good to hear from you.

Sincerely,

Sam Nunn

Sam Nunn

SN/nlu

PLEASE NOTE . . . this response was to a later letter. I received NO response regarding my health care concerns.

Contacting the President

IT IS MY PERSONAL BELIEF that it will do little good to write President Obama. I base this belief on the arrogant, condescending attitude he has shown during his multiple TV appearances, along with the comments he has made. Obama says what he thinks Americans want to hear, and then proceeds to encourage Congress to act in a completely opposite manner . . . one that will quickly move his liberal agenda forward. He truly is the quintessential politician, a master at double speak. On the health care issue he is guilty of outright lies and the sin of omission when "explaining" what health care reforms entail.

Now that I've said this, I must admit that I shall call, email, fax or write the President from time to time. It makes me feel better just to give him an earful . . . nicely, of course! I wonder if Obama will pull a Clinton at the end of his first year in office. Just a bit of history, for fun! Newspaper reports at the end of Clinton's first year reported that he received more calls, faxes, and letters in his first year in office than President George H. W. Bush received in his entire four year Presidency. The press reported the White House's breakdown of these contacts; there were six or seven categories. The first category on the list was the number of people who had contacted the President just to say they *loved* him. They also reported that none of the categories had ever had a single negative fax, call or letter in opposition to any of Clinton's programs. Obviously all of my letters, phone messages, and faxes were just put in the trash.

General Guidelines for Contacting the President

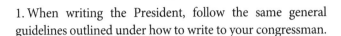

1. When writing the President, follow the same general guidelines outlined under how to write to your congressman.

2. Address the letter:
>   Dear Mr. President, or
>   Dear President Obama

3. The correct address:
>   President Barack Obama
>   The White House
>   1600 Pennsylvania Avenue
>   Washington, D.C. 20500

4. The White House Fax number is (202) 456-2461. This line is generally very busy during office hours so you may want to fax your comments in the evening.

5. The White House Comment Line number is: (202) 456-1111. This line stays extremely busy so *keep trying*. Office hours are 9–5 EST Monday–Friday. The direct WH number is: (202) 456-1414

6. *Do not speak harshly while giving your comments to the operator* . . . the line will be disconnected at once. Even "damn" counts . . . I know from my Clinton era experiences. Supposedly comments are summarized twice a day and then given directly to the President. Sure!

7. Unless things have changed, the Comments Line Operator should not ask you your name or address. The system is not supposed to give them your phone number. You might be asked for your state. I used to give them this

information, but decided it might be used to help the President when he runs for reelection, so now I refuse. In the next election he could use that type of information to campaign harder in states from which he had gotten lots of negative calls. Of course using information received this way would be illegal under federal law.

8. Maybe I'm wrong, but if we write, email, fax and call enough, maybe we'll finally convince this President and the Democrats that we don't want what they are selling. Naturally, Obama believes that he and his elitist friends know what we all need even if we're too dumb to realize what's good for us. Maybe we just need to double our efforts, turning out by the thousands at town hall meetings across the country and by flooding Washington with phones calls, emails, faxes and letters.

9. Do not expect a reply from the President that in any manner acknowledges that you are an individual person. I've gotten the same form letter twice and the same small thank you card twice. Only once did I get a personalized response from Clinton.

✍ Phone and Fax Lines at the White House

ALL AREA CODES (202)	FAX	PHONE
The White House Switchboard	456-2461	456-1414
The White House Comment Line	456-1111	
The President—Barack H. Obama		
(Dear Mr. President)	456-2168	
The Chief of Staff, Rahm Emanuel		
(Dear Mr. Emanuel)	456-6797	456-2883
The Vice President—Joseph Biden		
(Dear Vice President Biden)	456-2461	456-1414

President's email address: president@whitehouse.gov

Sample Letter to the President

*Note that the following sample letter was not really intended
to persuade anyone of anything, merely to give evidence
of vocal and vociferous opposition to the President's agenda
—and to give whoever actually read it an earful!
Sending it also made me feel a bit better.*

President Barack Obama
1600 Pennsylvania Avenue
Washington, DC 20500

March 20, 2009

Dear Mr. President:

I am one of the people in this country who *did not* vote for you, but I was willing to give you a chance until you presented your wasteful tax and spend budget, with all its' economic stimuli and bailouts. You had the opportunity to truly be a Great President, but you just reverted back to business as usual! Unless you and the Congress (under your leadership) get your priorities straight and run this country like any other business that has to stay within its budget, you will be remembered as **President Herbert Hoover II.**

As a country we must declare war on the federal deficit and not by raising taxes on the middle class and the so-called "rich" ($250,000.00+) If you think a $250,000.00 income makes one rich today, just try living in the real world where you must pay taxes at all levels of government, mortgage payments, home upkeep, transportation expenses, and college tuition and then see how rich you feel on that income.

Don't ask me to sacrifice anymore until you and the **Congress find ways to sacrifice**! Begin with cutting out government waste and pork. For more specific places to cut, just consult with the Congressional Republicans. Everything the government touches becomes a giant mess . . . how can any of you have the gall to tell us you want to run our businesses and our health care.

If we didn't have the federal deficit and its huge interest payments that are eating up more and more of the budget, just think what we could do for education, the working poor, the homeless and the uninsured, etc. How about some *delayed gratification*—pay off the deficit first, without new taxes, and then think of all the money you (the government) would have to spend on social programs without one new dime from hard working Americans. And now you have raised the national debt ceiling to **over twelve trillion dollars! Get Real!**

Be honest with the American people—let them know how bad the deficit has become. No more creative financing. Delay gratification for future gains. No publicity campaign is going to make us believe you or the Democrats in Congress. You've broken too many promises in the past. Show us you can balance your own budget first. **The American people are not stupid!**

The press loves a liberal, big spender, but don't start feeling too smug. I can tell you that **middle class America** is angry and we are not going to take any more!

You seem to be very good with "about faces"—why don't you do one now and go down in history as one of our greatest presidents since George Washington. President Clinton, tried your left-wing ideas and then realized the American people did not agree with them. He made an about face and went back to the center giving him 8 years in office. You should too.

Thank You,

Sharon Cooper
Sharon Cooper

P.S. It seems ironic to me that while other countries are moving away from their Marxist ideology as fast as possible, you want to lead the United States Government in a march toward greater and greater socialism!

Just the Fax

TODAY MANY PEOPLE PREFER to avoid the American mail system and transmit their thoughts and concerns almost immediately by means of emails or fax. The same guidelines as those for writing a letter to your legislator discussed earlier apply to any written message, regardless of its mode of transmission. Many times I use a fax or an email to send a simpler and shorter message, with no follow up.

For example, the day before the Senate's final vote on the 1993 budget, I faxed (no email was available at the time) the same short message to every Senator. Basically I asked each of them to vote "No" and not to saddle the American taxpayer with more taxes, only to have the money wasted by the Federal bureaucracy. That legislation passed by only one vote. One more "No" vote would have changed the course of history.

In this book I have included the fax numbers and email addresses of all U.S. Senators and Representatives. These numbers may change over time. If a number is no longer working, call the legislator's office and ask for the fax number or email address. Also, you may call the local office of the senator or representative and a staff member there can be of help. The legislator's local office will also take your comments on issues.

When using a fax, a cover sheet should identify the recipient, give your name, a fax number, an email address if available, how many pages (including cover sheet) are being sent. Note on the cover letter if you would like a response.

You can also be connected with any legislator's office in Washington by phoning the main congressional switchboard. The main phone number for both the House and Senate is (202) 224-3121. When the switchboard operator answers, ask to be connected with the legislator that you are trying to reach. Each legislator's direct phone line is listed in the back of this book, as well as the legislator's fax number and email address.

---★---

Sample Fax
(to Senator J. Johnston)

---★---

★URGENT DELIVERY★

JUST THE FAX

PLEASE DELIVER THE FOLLOWING
MATERIAL AS SOON AS POSSIBLE.

DATE: 5 August 1993

TO: Senator J. Bennett Johnston

FAX NUMBER: 202-555-1123

FROM: Sharon Cooper   770-555-6547

NUMBER OF PAGES: 1
(Including transmittal sheet)

Dear Senator Johnson,

We know the pressure from the White House must be terrible, but the people of your state and all Americans are worth a second vote of **no** on this tax bill. Thanks for your first **NO** vote!

Please no deals. . . . do not turn your back on us as others have done.

Sincerely,

Sharon Cooper

Sharon Cooper

Senator Johnston Replies . . .

United States Senate
Washington, D.C. 20510

August 23, 1993

Ms. Sharon Cooper

Dear Ms. Cooper,

Thank you for contacting my office to express your opposition to President Clinton's economic package.

While I support the President's deficit reduction goals, I believe that his plan to achieve them was flawed. The package he offered relied too heavily on taxes over spending cuts. I believe that the most effective way to reduce the deficit is to cut government spending. Louisiana taxpayers are already heavily burdened with taxes.

Earlier this year, I joined three of my colleagues in the Senate in offering a bipartisan alternative to the President's plan. Our plan eliminated the BTU tax originally included in the budget package, as well as the transportation fuels tax, and reversed the ratio of spending cuts to tax increases in the President's plan by providing $2 in spending cuts for every $1 in tax increases. I believe that this is the kind of tough but fair deficit reduction package that the American people want and need. Unfortunately, the Budget Reconciliation bill did not contain these provisions.

With kindest regards, I am

Sincerely,

J Bennett Johnston
J Bennett Johnston

★ Letters to the Editor ★

IN MANY WAYS, writing a letter to the editor is like writing a letter to your legislator and many of the same guidelines apply. However, in a letter to the editor you must be even more concise with your thoughts. You do have a little more leeway in being straightforward with your opinions. Just as with writing legislators, foul or abusive language of any sort or personal unpleasantness is a letter's ticket straight to the wastebasket.

For me it is also much more exciting to see a letter in print where hundreds, maybe thousands, of people may read what I wrote, than it is to only have one or two people in Washington reading a letter. This is not to downplay the significance of writing to congressmen. Both avenues of expressing your beliefs and concerns are important for each reaches very different audiences. Both are useful in the game of politics. I'm amazed at how many people read the editorial pages everyday. Except for the comics, the editorial section is the most widely read section in your newspaper; what a golden and underutilized opportunity to spread your message!

In our Atlanta paper most letters to the editor range between 150 and 200 words. Occasionally, there is a section for guest editorials and these are about triple the size of a letter to the editor.

🔆 Some ideas to keep in mind 🔆
when writing a letter to the editor:

1. Keep it simple. Keep it short.

2. Type the letter or make sure your handwriting is very legible. Double or triple space between lines to keep the editor happy.

3. No abusive language.

4. Humor and sarcasm can add a bit of spice, but just remember that too much spice can spoil any dish or letter.

5. Organize all of your thoughts carefully.

6. Limit the letter to one issue.

7. Give your reasons for writing in the very first sentence if possible.

8. Supply data supporting your view.

9. Close with a brief statement, question, or suggestion for action.

10. Most newspapers require that the writer provide a name, signature, address and daytime telephone number. Some editors also like to have a recent photo.

The newspaper staff may edit or condense your letter. I have included a letter to the editor as written by a friend, and then have included the edited version that was published.

Since each letter to the editor should be limited to one issue, you may want to submit several letters (only one at a time) for consideration. All papers like an exclusive so submit your letter to one paper, wait a week and if your letter has not been published, submit it to another paper. By observing the type of editorials printed in the different papers in your area, you should soon realize which papers are conservative and which are liberal. You should also notice the length of editorials each paper usually publishes so that you can make your letter conform to their format.

I have found that small daily or weekly newspapers are often hungry for copy, so you may find it easier to get your viewpoints in print in their publications rather than in large syndicated papers. These small papers are very important to their communities and often more closely read than the large papers.

Typically you will find directions for writing and submitting your letters to the editor in the editorial section itself. Any specific rules, such as a required signature, will also be listed along with the paper's fax number, email address and mailing address. When in a hurry to make my opinions public, I email my letter. Don't forget to include your return address, email address, fax number and phone number.

Remember if at first you don't succeed at having your letter to the editor published . . . try, try and try again.

Sample Submitted Letter
to the Editor

21 April 1993

The Atlanta Constitution
Letters to the Editor
72 Marietta Street
Atlanta, Georgia 30303

Dear Editor,

President Clinton reported that he and Hillary "took a pretty good lick" on the 15th. They paid $70,228 in taxes on an adjusted gross income of $290,697. To start with, doesn't this six-figure income make them part of the greedy "economic elite," whom they're constantly blaming for America's problems?

Furthermore, Arkansas taxpayers last year provided the Clintons with housing, food, health care, and almost all their other necessities. This means that Bill and Hillary had more than $200,000, after taxes, to spend on luxuries or to sock away for the future!

No wonder the Clintons are so out of touch with America—and no wonder they think that paying more taxes is no problem. Maybe someone should tell these two hypocrites that some of us out here have to actually try to live on the money we make.

Sincerely,

Eric Bowles
Eric Bowles

Read the published version of the above letter on the next page and see if you can find what editors at the paper deleted before publication.

133

Same Sample as Published

(Printed in the 𝕬𝖙𝖑𝖆𝖓𝖙𝖆 𝕮𝖔𝖓𝖘𝖙𝖎𝖙𝖚𝖙𝖎𝖔𝖓)

CLINTON'S TAXES MERE PEANUTS

DEAR EDITOR:

President Clinton reported that he and Hillary "took a pretty good lick" on the 15th. They paid $70,228 in taxes on an adjusted gross income of $290,697. To start with, doesn't this six-figure income make them part of the greedy "economic elite," whom they're constantly blaming for America's problems?

Furthermore, Arkansas taxpayers last year provided the Clintons with housing, food, health care, and almost all their other necessities. This means that Bill and Hillary had more than $200,000, after taxes, to spend on luxuries or to sock away for the future!

No wonder the Clintons are so out of touch.

Eric Bowles
Marietta

CLINTON'S TAXES MERE PEANUTS
DEAR EDITOR:

President Clinton reported that he and Hillary "took a pretty good lick" on the 15th. They paid $70,228 in taxes on an adjusted gross income of $290,697. To start with, doesn't this six-figure income make them part of the greedy "economic elite," whom they're constantly blaming for America's problems?

Furthermore, Arkansas taxpayers last year provided the Clintons with housing, food, health care, and almost all their other necessities. This means that Bill and Hillary had more than $200,000, after taxes, to spend on luxuries or to sock away for the future!

No wonder the Clintons are so out of touch.

Eric Bowles
Marietta

Hold Your Very Own Taxpayer's Tea Party

★ Be a Taxpayer with Attitude! ★

"Politics ought to be the part-time profession of every citizen who would protect the rights and privileges of free people and who would preserve what is good and fruitful in our national heritage"
—Dwight D. Eisenhower

The whole purpose of this book is to motivate you, a hardworking American Taxpayer, to become involved. It has become absolutely critical for you to take an active role in your government. Liberal tax-and-spend politicians, especially those in Washington, have failed us. Our country has reached the point where apparently only everyday citizens can apply the kind of shock therapy needed to set things straight. Some kind of radical, yet peaceful, action is required. It is time for more and more Tea Parties.

Get busy, gather with your friends and family and have your own Tea Parties. For example you could stage a peaceful protest, attend a town hall meeting, hold a petition drive or hold a voter registration blitz. As you become more involved you may want to spend your own money to hire a billboard (if you live in a rural area they typically go for reasonable prices), air radio ads, or even pay for a TV commercial. As long as you spend only your money, express your own views on a particular issue (or a bill), or suggest that people call their congressman you do not have a spending limit or any reporting requirements. **Don't ask anyone's permission! It's your country and you're the Boss.** (Just keep it legal.)

Please note, the demeanor of attendees at town hall meetings has gotten a lot of attention in the media. When topics are very personal to citizens, they often have trouble holding back their emotions. In any large gathering it is important to have a sense of order if there is to be any real exchange of ideas. Once someone begins yelling most people tune them out immediately. Just like in writing a letter, when it is your turn to speak, speak clearly, be polite, well organized (write your thoughts down before hand) and speak from the heart.

Speaking of keeping it legal: if you specifically advocate the election or defeat of any federal official there are strict reporting requirements and very specific guidelines that must be followed. This type of action is considered to be an independent expenditure; there is a specific section in this book pertaining to these expenditures.

A way to motivate friends who think they are not interested in the political process is to give them a copy of this book. Humor can be a great teacher and Chuck Asay's cartoons make it clear why people must become involved. Infect your friends with your enthusiasm; make things happen. This book is jammed with ideas and information calculated to give tax'n spend legislators a serious pain in the election. That doesn't mean your own ideas might not be even better. So if you have a good idea, spread it around! You aren't being graded.

Most important of all, do something now! We aren't going to get out of this mess by sitting on our duffs. I've gotten off of mine; you should get off of yours, too. Maybe you're not ready to take matters entirely into your own hands but you can still make a significant difference in the democratic process. Outlined below are two great entry-level ways of participating.

★ DONATING TO A CAMPAIGN ★

Donating to a campaign is such an easy way to help that it almost doesn't count. Money is the lifeblood of any campaign. Radio and

TV ads, office rent, telephone lines, gas, filing fees, and salaries for paid staff all add up to a cost of hundreds of thousands of dollars, if not millions, for a federal campaign. Thank goodness state races are typically less expensive. DON'T PANIC—donations of $25, $50, or $100 still make up the vast majority of donations.

If you have found a candidate you can believe in, either in your district or anywhere else in the country, your donation will help them get their message out and help them beat a tax and spend liberal. Remember though, the federal law sets specific limits on how much you can donate. Limits for state candadates vary from state to state. Candidates know what their limits are and post them on their website or print them in their campaign literature.

Here are the current federal limits in a nutshell: You can donate up to $2,400 to a single federal candidate for a primary election and up to an additional $2,400 per candidate in a general election. You may not donate more than $45,600 total to all federal candidates in a single year. There is also a yearly limit of $69,900 that you can donate to federal PACS such as the National Senatorial Campaign Committee and the National Republican Congressional Campaign Committee.

★ VOLUNTEERING IN A CAMPAIGN ★

If money is the lifeblood, volunteers are the backbone of any campaign. Giving of your time is not only a great way to make a difference in an election, but it gives you a chance to build a relationship with the candidate. When you back the winner, you will then have someone in Washington or at your state capitol who is much more likely to listen and carefully consider your viewpoint on issues.

It doesn't take any special skills to be a volunteer. If you can stuff envelopes, answer the phone, type labels, or put up yard signs you are well qualified. Other specialized skills such as bookkeeping, writing, photography or specific computer skills may also be put to use.

The amount of time you volunteer is up to you. Even one hour spent helping to get a mailing ready can be very helpful. Perhaps you could donate one afternoon a week on a regular basis. Or if your time is limited, you could ask to be called in to help with special projects. Campaigns have many events on the weekends such as neighborhood canvassing drives, fund-raisers and rallies. Volunteers are needed to make all of these events a success.

Getting involved in a campaign is not hard—like swimming, just jump in. Call or go by a candidate's campaign headquarters. You probably won't find the campaign's address and phone number in the phone book. Many candidates open campaign offices early in the election year and close down soon after the Election Day. Look in the candidate's campaign literature to find the campaign address and phone number or try searching the Internet since most campaigns have a website.

At the campaign office, ask for either the campaign manager or the volunteer coordinator and offer your services. Even if your services are not needed right that moment, they will take your contact information and the next time volunteers are needed you should receive a call. Some campaigns are less organized than others, so if you do not get a call back in a reasonable amount of time, be persistent and call the campaign back.

Every campaign has different needs, but here are a few examples of routine volunteer activities:

- ✔ **Fold newsletters**
- ✔ **Distribute yard signs**
- ✔ **Make phone calls reminding people to vote**
- ✔ **Recruit volunteers**
- ✔ **Serve food at a fund-raiser**
- ✔ **Pick up out of town speakers at the airport**
- ✔ **Deliver ads to radio and TV stations**
- ✔ **Transport dignitaries**
- ✔ **Go door to door delivering campaign material**

During the election season there are hundreds of jobs that will need to be done; a campaign will welcome your participation on any level.

Sample 60-Second Radio Ad

President Obama thinks that
you don't pay enough for electricity.

Congressman John Henson agrees with him.

President Obama wants to raise
your monthly electric bill by almost 50%.

Congressman John Henson thinks that's okay.

President Obama wants to raise
natural gas prices by 55%.

Congressman John Henson feels
that's what's best for Americans.

President Obama wants to raise gasoline prices by 58%

Congressman John Henson believes Obama is right.

On June 26, your congressman, John Henson
voted for the Cap and Trade Act.
This is an indirect tax on all hardworking Americans.
Call (202) 555-5555 and send
Congressman Henson a message . . .
No more taxes, direct or indirect.

★

President Obama, Congressman Henson and higher
taxes: Some things just seem to go together.

**Paid for by Suzie Jenkins,
a hard working American Taxpayer.**

***Please note:** Radio ads are easier and cheaper to make than one would think and it is really fun to hear yourself on the air. Since only an issue (no more taxes) was being pushed in the above ad, the cost would not have to be reported no matter how how many times it aired. If the ad had advocated that Congressman Henson be defeated in the election or if the ad mentioned an opponent it would then be an independent expenditure and therefore would have to be reported. (See the following section for the rules pertaining to independent expenditures.)

A Secret Weapon: Independent Expenditures

GIVEN THE STATE OF OUR ECONOMY, if you are one of those exceedingly rare individuals with a significant amount of disposable income after paying all of your bills and taxes and you have reached the legal limits for contributions to federal candidates, but still want to do more . . . there is a way, via independent expenditures.

An independent expenditure is an expenditure for a communication "expressly advocating the election or defeat of a clearly identified candidate that is not made in cooperation, consultation, or concert with, or at the request or suggest of, a candidate, a candidate's authorized committee, or their agents, or a political party or its agents." *11 CFR 100.16(a)*. If the communication is coordinated or made at the request or suggestion of a candidate, candidate's committee or party or any of their agents, it is then considered a coordinated communication and thus becomes an in-kind contribution that must stay within the contribution limits put forth by the federal campaign finance law.

An individual making an independent expenditure must file a report with the FEC on FEC Form 5 at the end of the first reporting period in which independent expenditures with respect to a given election aggregate more than $250 in a calendar year and in any succeeding period during the same year in which additional independent expenditure of any amount are made. *11 CFR 109.10(b)*

In a nutshell: if you make independent expenditures that total more than $249.99 per candidate in one calendar year you must report. To learn more about independent expenditures and the disclaimer requirements on such communication please consult the brochure, *COORDINATED COMMUNICATIONS AND INDE-PENDENT EXPENDITURE.* In addition you may access FEC Form 5 and accompanying instructions from the FEC website which is FEC.gov. You can also contact staff in the Information Division at the FEC by calling toll free 1-800-424-9530 and press 6 when prompted.

DO NOT BE DISCOURAGED. I have a final word for those who find that the above has had a chilling effect on your desire to participate financially in the political process of their country. *Independent Expenditures less than $250 are not subject to any reporting requirements* and $249.99 will buy quite a few bumper stickers, yard signs, wee hour radio spots, and many other products for advocating your position on a political campaign.

Just remember that to keep expenditures independent, you must NOT coordinate with any candidate or campaign committee—don't even stop by for a pat on the head afterwards. **Also you must include the following statement in any communication: "Paid for by (your name) and not authorized by any candidate or committee."** Don't fret, that is easy to include on bumper stickers, signs, and whatever else you can buy for less than $250.

In the spirit of John Lennon's song: Just imagine what would happen if a million or fifty million or one hundred million outraged taxpayers each spent $249.99 on throwing those Washington rascals out. Imagine . . .

Vote—You Have Nothing to Lose But Your Congressman!

APPARENTLY DEMOCRAT POLITICIANS in Washington, along with a few misguided Republicans, have been struck DEAF, DUMB AND BLIND! They believe the public's expression of disgust for their proposed policies at town hall meetings is just the rantings of "right wing nuts" or racists. They refuse to acknowledge that approximately one hundred thousand everyday Americans were mad enough to travel to Washington on September 12, 2009 to protest their runaway spending and their proposed health care changes. And, worst of all, the Democrats seem to have lost their ability to speak for themselves, following their far left liberal leaders like little lemmings. No longer do they listen to and speak for the citizens in their districts, the very ones who elected them to office in the first place.

There is a solution . . . we must VOTE THE RASCALS OUT OF OFFICE! Of course, the politicians in Washington think they are in safe districts, or that the American people will soon lose interest in what's happening. By next election season Democrats believe voters will be complacent once more and all their "sins" will be forgotten. Boy are they wrong. A sleeping giant, the American taxpayer has been awakened and is mad as Hell.

The day to remember will be November 10, 2010. That is the first opportunity worried and upset Americans will have to express their frustrations in a very concrete way. All members of the U.S. House of Representatives and one third of those in the U.S. Senate will stand for re-election on that day. By voting out of office those that have not listened and who have voted for left wing policies and tax and spend bills, middle-class Americans will have taken a major step in reclaiming our country, a country based on freedom, personal accountability and fiscal responsibility.

For too long everyday Americans didn't pay attention to what was happening in Washington. I know, because I was one of them! Politicians learned that they could say and act one way back in their home district and then vote exactly opposite in D.C. Thank goodness those days are over. Every bill that's introduced in Congress and every vote that's taken is being closely watched and, thanks to the Internet and Fox News, that information is readily available to all Americans.

Washington politicians must be taught that we are not a country that leans to the radical left, or for that matter, to the far right. We also do not like rapid change and we don't want to be spent into bankruptcy. To finally drive this message home, concerned citizens will have to show up at the polls next November in droves. By voting to send a number of the current Washington tax and spend rascals packing, the others won't be so quick to dismiss the concerns of their constituents in the future.

Get ready—November 2, 2010 will be here before you know it!
★ BE PREPARED: ★

REGISTER TO VOTE and get everyone who thinks like you to register also. Some states drop people from their voter rolls if the person does not vote in a number of elections. Make sure your registration is current. If you have moved, you also need to notify the registrar, so that you can be given the address of your correct voting location. For information on how to check on any of the above, call or go to your state's secretary of state website, or your county or parish election board.

Register now, because in most states you cannot just show up on Election Day, register on the spot and then vote. States usually have a cut-off date for registering before elections, for both primaries and general elections. Make sure you know that date, better yet, just register now. If you keep on voting, you only have to go register once.

Don't believe the old wives' tale' that you are going to be called for jury duty just because you have registered to vote. In order to get a diverse jury pool, states now use a variety of lists, such as property tax records and drivers license records, to call citizens to jury duty.

Primary elections are important! Some politicians believe they are safe because the district they represent leans so far Democrat, or so far Republican, the candidate from the opposite party can't win. They can however, get a primary challenge from someone in their own party. A brand new congressman can't be any worse than a known bad one. Make sure you pay attention and vote in the primaries too.

Every vote counts, so on election day, don't just vote yourself, but make sure your friends and family also vote. Drive them to the polls if necessary.

★ ★ ★

*P.S. A WORD OF CAUTION: As appealing as it may seem, a vote for any independent party candidate is a vote for the candidate you want to lose. At this point in our history we are still a two party system, and an independent candidate is only a spoiler, something we can't afford in 2010. Republicans are certainly not perfect, but they are not nearly as bad as the Democrats in power now. Like I said earlier, even though Republicans missed some golden opportunities while in control, I think they've learned their lessons. If not, you can throw them out too in the very next election cycle.

Until November 2, 2010, when you can exercise the most valuable right you possess as a citizen of the United States, your vote, you can't just sit back on your laurels. Concerned citizens must continue to voice their opposition to their elected officials in Washington in a loud and clear manner. Also, candidates who challenge an incumbent are going to need help from all of us. Incumbents always have the advantage, especially money-wise. So get involved. Give what you can and work like mad for your candidate. We cannot let up the pressure.

Information Shared is
Information Multiplied

EARLIER I MENTIONED that I clip interesting and informative articles from many sources. I then use them to clarify my own thinking, and to help in my crusade to encourage my friends, my husband's patients and virtually anybody else who will listen to me to call their elected officials for or against my issue of the day. Unquestionably, Americans would be a lot better off with lower taxes and less government intrusion into our lives. Did you think that I wouldn't try to share my passions and sources with you? And don't you forget to share them with your friends! One of my best resources during the Clinton Health Care debate was an article from *Reader's Digest*. It gave a realistic and fairly negative evaluation of the British Single Payer health system. Since *Reader's Digest* has the reputation of being unbiased, I ordered reprints of this article (dirt cheap in large quantities) and gave them out to everyone I knew. With today's Internet sources, there are hundreds of excellent resources just a click away. I want to thank all of my sources, including Newt Gingrich, Americans for Tax Reform and all others mentioned in this book. The websites listed will provide you with massive amounts of reliable and sensible information.

Cost of Government Day
(COGD) 2008

ACCORDING TO AMERICANS FOR TAX REFORM the Cost of Government Day "is the date Americans have earned enough in gross wages to pay off their share of the combined cost of taxes, government spending and regulation. Cost of Government Day incorporates government spending (as opposed to just taxes), federal regulatory costs and some state regulatory cost."

Cost of Government Day for 2009 was August 12. That means that hard working Americans had to toil an average of *224 days* in 2009 just to "Pay the Bill" imposed on them by the government. *Americans had to work 27 days longer in 2009 than in 2008.* For the record Americans had to work 44 days longer in 2009 than they did in 2000 when the COGD fell on June 29. Who knows how long we will be working for the Government instead of our families and ourselves if the President and current members of Congress get their way and pass all of the new mega spending programs that they are trying to force down the taxpayer's throat.

Since the Obama Administration took office in late January' 09 the federal deficit has increased 1.267 trillion dollars and by the end of the 2009 it is estimated that it will reach 1.84 trillion. That will be the largest one-year increase in the national debt in our nation's history. Now the Treasury Secretary is asking for Congress to raise the debt ceiling to over fourteen trillion dollars. The new health care plan that is being proposed by the President and the Democrats has a cost estimate of 900 billion to 1.6 trillion over the next 10 years—and when did any government program come in as estimated? The White House said that it is demanding cost saving measures from all agencies and made a big to do recently about the 100 million savings that had been realized. To us that is a lot of money, but in the Federal budget that equals a fraction of one percent. One department bragged on their big idea for cost savings—they are now beginning to print on both sides of a piece of paper.

★ Job Loss and Economic Decline ★

WHILE THERE IS NO WAY to know the exact effect that higher taxes and bigger government will have on our already weakened economy, most economist are in agreement that jobs will be lost. Nationwide the unemployment rate is now almost 10% and some states have much higher rates than that—with the expectation of even more job losses before the economy turns around. Estimates of total job losses as a result of higher taxes range from the hundred of thousands to millions. Some economists believe that there will be no new sustainable jobs created during the next five years. Think what that means just to young people graduating from college. Increased taxes in this economy will have a devastating effect on supply and demand.

Taxes on fuels and income will reduce spending power. There will be less demand for products, fewer goods sold, and fewer workers needed. Taxes on corporations and incomes will reduce the amount of money available for venture capital and will reduce profit margins. It will be necessary to lay off workers, increase prices and reduce wages.

This administration needs to take note of the fact that in the last 30 years there have only been two periods in which Americans enjoyed a significant reduction in the number of days that they had to work to pay their cost of government bill. Both of these declines resulted from a combination of restraining the growth of government and letting private enterprise flourish, allowing the economy and national income to grow.

———————★———————

A Pro Jobs, Pro Growth Plan for Health Reform

———————★———————

by Newt Gingrich and Nancy Desmond

AMERICA DESPERATELY NEEDS REAL CHANGE in our health and healthcare system. Americans are paying more and more money for less and less quality care.

At the Center for Health Transformation, we have been working for the past six years to develop solutions for the problems in our health care system, which don't rely on higher taxes, bigger government, and more bureaucrats.

We believe we can have a system in which every American has access to better health with more choices at lower cost.

We believe we can have a system in which the individual and his or her doctor have the knowledge and incentives to make wise choices; a system in which fraud and waste are rooted out, in which quality and best practices (not volume of services) are rewarded and in which prevention, health and wellness are central.

And most importantly in today's troubled economy, we believe we can have a system that will also be central to job creation and to America's economic recovery.

★ Six Straightforward Steps to Better Healthcare ★

**To create a system that delivers more choices of
higher quality health care at lower cost we need to take
the following six straightforward steps:**

1. *Stop Paying the Crooks.* First, we must dramatically
   reduce healthcare fraud within our current healthcare
   system. Outright fraud—criminal activity—accounts for
   as much as 10 percent of all healthcare spending. That is
   more than $200 billion every year. Medicare alone could
   account for as much as $40 billion a year. (Read about our
   latest CHT Press book, *Stop Paying the Crooks*, edited by
   Jim Frogue.)

2. *Move from a Paper-based to an Electronic Health System.*
   As it stands now, it is simply impossible to keep up with
   fraud in a paper-based system. An electronic system
   would free tens of billions of dollars to be spent on
   investing in the kind of modern system that will transform
   healthcare. In addition, it would dramatically increase our
   ability to eliminate costly medical errors and to accelerate
   the adoption of new solutions and breakthroughs.

3. *Tax Reform.* The savings realized through very deliberately
   and very systematically eliminating fraud could be used to
   provide tax incentives and vouchers that would help cover
   those Americans who currently can't afford coverage.
   In addition, we need to expand tax incentives for insurance
   provided by small employers and the self-employed.
   Finally, elimination of capital gains taxes for investments
   in health-solution companies can greatly impact the
   creation and advancement of new solutions that create
   better health at lower cost.

4. *Create a Health-Based Health System.* In essence, we must create a system that focuses on improving individual health. The best way to accomplish this is to find out what solutions are actually working today that save lives and save money and then design public policy to encourage their widespread adoption. For example, according to the Dartmouth Health Atlas, if the 6,000 hospitals in the country provided the same standard of care of the Intermountain or Mayo health clinics, Medicare alone would save 30 percent of total spending every year. We need to make best practices the minimum practice. We need the federal government and other healthcare stakeholders to consistently migrate to best practices that ensure quality, safety and better outcomes.

5. *Reform Our Health Justice System.* Currently, the U.S. civil justice system is the most expensive in the world— about double the average cost in virtually every other industrialized nation. But for all of the money spent, our civil justice system neither effectively compensates persons injured from medical negligence nor encourages the elimination of medical errors. Because physicians fear malpractice suits, defensive medicine (redundant, wasteful treatment designed to avoid lawsuits, not treat the patient) has become pervasive. CHT is developing a number of bold health-justice reforms including a "safe harbor" for physicians who followed clinical best practices in the treatment of a patient. Visit CHT's Health Justice project page to learn more.

6. *Invest in Scientific Research and Breakthroughs.* We must accelerate and focus national efforts, reengineer care delivery, and ultimately prevent diseases such as Alzheimer's disease and diabetes, which are financially crippling our healthcare system.

★ The Last Thing We Need is a Plan ★
That Raises Taxes and Eliminates Jobs

CLEARLY, THE LAST THING AMERICA NEEDS is a healthcare plan that will raise taxes, eliminate jobs, and allows Washington bureaucrats to make decisions that ought to be made by individual Americans together with their families and doctors.

We can make health and healthcare into a major source of job creation, economic revival, and improved health and well being for every American.

Or we can make it into a government-run system that will destroy our economy along with our health.

To learn more about our plan for reforming health without raising taxes, eliminating jobs or raising the deficit, please visit www.healthtransformation.net.

"A Pro Jobs, Pro Growth Plan for Health Reform" reprinted with kind permission from the authors.

━━━★━━━
American Solutions for Winning the Future
━━★━━
Endorsement of Twelve American Solutions for Jobs and Prosperity

1. *Payroll Tax Stimulus.* With a temporary new tax credit to offset 50% of the payroll tax, every small business would have more money, and all Americans would take home more of what they earned.

2. *Real Middle-Income Tax Relief.* Reduce the marginal tax rate of 25% down to 15%, in effect establishing a flat-rate tax of 15% for close to 9 out of 10 American workers.

3. *Reduce the Business Tax Rate.* Match Ireland's rate of 12.5% to keep more jobs in America.

4. *Homeowner's Assistance.* Provide tax credit incentives to responsible homebuyers so they can keep their homes.

5. *Control Spending So We Can Move to a Balanced Budget.* This begins with eliminating Congressional earmarks and wasteful pork-barrel spending.

6. *No State Aid Without Protection From Fraud.* Require state governments to adopt anti-fraud and anti-theft policies before giving them more money.

7. *More American Energy Now.* Explore for more American oil and gas and invest in affordable energy for the future, including clean coal, ethanol, nuclear power and renewable fuels.

8. *Abolish Taxes on Capital Gains.* Match China, Singapore and many other competitors. More investment in America means more jobs in America.

9. *Protect the Rights of American Workers.* We must protect a worker's right to decide by secret ballot whether to join a union, and a worker's right to negotiate freely. Forced unionism will kill jobs at a time when we can't afford to lose them.

10. *Replace Sarbanes-Oxley.* This failed law is crippling entrepreneurial startups. Replace it with affordable rules that help create jobs, not destroy them.

11. *Abolish the Death Tax.* Americans should work for their families, not for Washington.

12. *Invest in Energy and Transportation Infrastructure.* This includes a new, expanded electric power grid and a 21st century air traffic control system that will reduce delays in air travel and save passengers, employees and airlines billions of dollars per year.

footnote: The Twelve American Solutions For Jobs and Prosperity are reprinted courtesy of American Solutions. 1425 K Street, NW, Suite 750, Washington, DC 20005. Website: www.americansolutions.com

Gangster Government

How Obama and the Democrats Have Robbed Americans of Their Money and Freedom

☛ *$787 Federal Stimulus*—The Democrats in Congress adopted the biggest spending bill in American history in almost utter secrecy. It was unveiled the night before the vote in the House and Senate, giving the elected representatives of the people NO TIME to read the 1,100 page bill. The so-called tax relief for middle and low-income workers in the plan equals $13 a week this year and $8 a week in 2010. The rest is spend, spend, spend. *On April 15, the day all of us have to file returns to the IRS, Obama said, "My administration has taken far-reaching action to give tax cuts to the Americans who need them."* Really? One advocacy group ran ads reminding us you could spend $1 million a day for every day back to the day Jesus walked the earth and you still wouldn't have spent as much as the Democrats will spend on a bailout that has done nothing to turn around the economy.

☛ *Czars*—Let's talk about expansion of government in proportions we have never seen in our lifetime. Obama not only has a traditional Cabinet but he has 31 czars including the auto czar, TARP czar, climate czar, pay czar, urban affairs czar and a czar on the Sudan. *The Obama White House actually has more czars than the Romanovs did in their entire lineage.* CNBC's Larry Kudlow recently documented that many of these czars were big contributors to the Democratic Party and the 2008 Obama campaign including the pay czar who gave $23,800 and the car czar who donated $61,000.

☛ *Second Stimulus*—With unemployment stuck at almost 10 percent, White House economists are now saying a second stimulus is a must. Remember Obama said the first package would keep unemployment at 8 percent or less? The largest holder of U.S. bonds, the Chinese, *LAUGHED* at Treasury Secretary Timothy Geithner when he gave an address saying the dollar is secure. Geithner said the Democrats would be "very disciplined" in fiscal and budgetary matters in the future. Really?

☛ *Auto Bailout*—The President's takeover of GM and Chrysler included strong language that he does not want to run the auto makers. Yet the deals he brokered prohibited GM, for example, from importing cars it makes at its overseas plants. *Obama fired the CEO of GM and appointed new members to the board including union members—the very unions that drove the automakers into bankruptcy.* The Administration also has mandated fuel efficiency standards for new cars, telling automakers what kind of vehicles they must design in the future. *"The government will not interfere with or exert control over day-to-day company operations," Obama said.* Rep. Barney Frank and others have lobbied both automakers on recent corporate decisions. *Is this government staying out of the car business?*

☛ *Charitable Tax Deductions*—The Obama proposal for the 2010 budget originally called for eliminating tax deductions for those who can afford to donate the most to charities—the wealthy. This would have eliminated an incentive for high-net worth people, including the Bill Gates of the world, to maintain their philanthropic giving. Many, many charities would have suffered or collapsed because of it. The idea was dropped.

☛ *Silencing Critics*—Despite the Administration's claims that the EPA would make environmental policy based on science, the EPA recently silenced a senior analyst for research that seriously questioned the science behind global warming. Alan Carlin, a 35-year veteran of the agency's National Center for Environmental Economics, was told to shut up and not conduct any more research on the subject after issuing a 98-page analysis arguing the agency should take another look since the science was inconclusive at best. *How ironic when Obama said in April, "The days of science taking a back seat to ideology are over."* An EPA official told Carlin in an April email obtained by the American Enterprise Institute: "You need to move on to other issues and subjects. I don't want you to spend any additional EPA time on climate change. No papers, no research etc . . ." Obama also recently fired the Inspector General of the Corporation for National Community Service (which oversees volunteers and community organizing) for policy disagreements.

☛ *Deficits*—Just three months after adopting the $787 billion stimulus that has printing presses running 24/7, Speaker Nancy Pelosi gave an interview in which *Pelosi said, "We inherited the debt from the Bush administration, an unconscionable, almost immoral, obscene debt."* This after she rammed through an almost $1 trillion spending spree that taxpayers couldn't even read online despite the Obama White House and Democrats pledging to be more "transparent" than their Republican counterparts. THE NUMBERS: Despite Bush's Medicare prescription drug benefit and other items which expanded the federal budget by $700 billion, Obama will surpass him by adding over $1 trillion in debt his FIRST YEAR IN OFFICE ALONE *excluding* a proposed new government health program.

☛ *Pork Chops*—The Republican Congress may have been accused of building a "bridge to nowhere," and other pork projects, but the new Federal stimulus just approved by the Democrats has more than its fair share of bacon. Items include: $886,000 for a disc golf course in Austin; $6 million for a snowmaking machine at a resort in Duluth, Minnesota; $150 million for parking improvements at a little league facility in Puerto Rico; $200 million for a new Homeland Security Headquarters; $8 billion for new rail projects including one from Las Vegas to Los Angeles to serve Harry Reid; $200 million to re-sod the Mall in Washington; and $200 million to buy an "ice breaker" ship to sail through the North Pole. *Saying "We passed the recovery plan free of earmarks," Obama and Democrats then adopted a budget with 9,000 earmarks, according to* Time *magazine. Harry Reid's response to the pork? "We cannot let spending be done by a bunch of nameless, faceless bureaucrats buried in this town someplace."*

☛ *Media*—Sensing the "love affair" may be in jeopardy, the White House has resorted to manipulating some in the press. It has been pre-screening reporters prior to press conferences, letting pre-approved reporters know they will be the ones to ask questions at the Presidential press conferences. The Huffington Post even agreed to ask a question requested by the White House at a recent press conference, and there have been questions raised about the pre-selection of questions asked at these supposedly open town hall meetings. White House press corps matriarch Helen Thomas, 89, confronted press secretary Robert Gibbs saying, "I am amazed at you people who call for openness and transparency." *In an interview with CBS, Thomas said "Who the hell do they think we are, puppets?"* If only the rest of the press corps had her integrity.

☛ *Terrorists*—Because he is too proud to reverse an order made without research, Obama has had a difficult time finding a place to send prisoners from the Guantanamo Bay prison he vowed to close by year's end. In fact, *three Chinese prisoners known as Uighurs got a one-way resettlement ticket to a beachside cottage on the island of Bermuda courtesy of the U.S. taxpayer.* Fox News just reported that a senior Taliban fighter recently released was identified in Afghanistan back fighting American soldiers. Obama wants to close Guantanamo, giving some terrorists a chance to head back to the battlefield to kill Americans. *Speaker Nancy Pelosi called the President's plan is "a sensible treatment of detainees."* Now Obama wants to try the 911 terrorist and give them the same legal rights as American Citizens,

☛ *Cap and Tax*—The House barely adopted this energy tax measure just before the July 4 recess. A 300-page amendment to the bill was submitted at 3 A.M. before voting began that day. *Co-sponsor Rep. Henry Waxman admitted, "I certainly don't claim to know everything that's in this bill. I don't know the details. I rely on the scientists."* According to the Heritage Foundation, a family of four would pay $436 more in energy costs and $1,241 a year more by 2035 under the proposal—all to discourage energy use in hopes of the U.S. having a dent alone on global warming. Electricity costs would climb 90 percent, natural gas 55 percent and gasoline 58 percent. *All total the tax hike would be $20,000 on a family of four by 2035. Despite the Democratic spin, this is NOT A JOBS bill. Every industry will have to charge more to produce and ship products from books sold on Amazon to farmers who grow corn and ship it to Publix; which will costs jobs. Obama called the bill "a bold and necessary step." Pelosi called it "transformational legislation that takes us into the future."*

☛ *Vegas*—During a town hall meeting, Obama blasted companies that had received federal bailout funds for ever having had conventions in Las Vegas and said they should never meet in Vegas in the future. That prompted the mayor of Las Vegas to demand an apology, especially since the city is suffering from a setback in tourism. *"He owes us an apology," said Mayor Oscar Goodman.* Obama never apologized, even though he had won Nevada in the 2008 election.

☛ *Taxes*—The Bush tax cuts of 2001 and 2003 reduced income tax rates for all tax brackets and set new, lower income tax rates for lower-income workers. Set to expire in 2011, the Democrats likely will not renew the tax cuts and will instead let your taxes rise to cover some of their massive spending. The results? After the $2 trillion Bush tax cuts, the stock marked surged 32 percent, the economy created 1.8 million jobs in the first 18 months then another 5.2 million jobs in the following 27 months. *Obama's plans will raise taxes $1.4 trillion in a climate where we are at almost 10 percent unemployment and a stock market that has dropped off a cliff from the 14,000 mark. All of us will see our income tax brackets increase.*

───★─── Vulnerable Democrats ───★───

AT THE END OF EVERY YEAR the National Taxpayer's Union rates all of the Congress by calculating which votes affected taxes, spending or the national debt, and then assigning a weight based on the importance of the vote which then yields the percentages as seen below. The list below represents all Democrat seats in the U.S. House whose district was won by John McCain. Clearly, by their NTU scores they do not seem to be friends of the taxpayer—*and if that was not enough, every Representative listed voted for the Cap and Trade Bill.*

The * denotes that McCain and Obama received 49% each in a district but ultimately McCain won the district. The ** denotes that the representative is a freshman and has not been evaluated by the National Taxpayer's Union.

Please Note . . . even if their leadership allowed them to vote against Obamacare because they were in vulnerable districts, their presence in Congress still helps the Democrats maintain their majority and allows Nancy Pelosi to remain Speaker. **Let's send them all packing on November 2, 2010!**

National Tax Union Chart

Name	District	Obamacare Yes/No Vote	% of Vote Received McCain	NTU Score/ Grade
Rep. Bobby Bright	AL-2	N	63%	N/A**
Rep. Parker Griffith	AL-5	N	61%	N/A**
Rep. Ann Kirkpatrick	AZ-1	Y	54%	N/A**
Rep. Harry Mitchell	AZ-5	Y	51%	31% /D
Rep. Gabrielle Giffords	AZ-8	Y	52%	19% /F
Rep. Marion Berry	AR-1	N	59%	6% /F
Rep. Vic Snyder	AR-2	Y	54%	7% /F
Rep. Mike Ross	AR-4	N	58%	7% /F
Rep. John Salazar	CO-3	Y	50%	14% /F
Rep. Betsy Markey	CO-4	Y	50%	N/A**
Rep. Allen Boyd Jr.	FL-2	Y	54%	13% /F
Rep. Suzanne Kosmas	FL-24	Y	51%	N/A**
Rep. Jim Marshall	GA-8	N	56%	22% /F
Rep. Walt Minnick	ID-1	N	62%	N/A**
Rep. Brad Ellsworth	IN-8	Y	51%	15% /F
Rep. Baron Hill	IN-9	Y	50%	22% /F
Rep. Ben Chandler	KY-6	N	55%	15% /F
Rep. Charlie Melancon	LA-3	N	61%	8% /F
Rep. Frank Kratovil Jr.	MD-1	N	59%	N/A**
Rep. Collin Peterson	MN-7	N	50%	21% /F
Rep. Travis Childers	MS-1	N	62%	31% /D
Rep. Gene Taylor	MS-4	N	67%	N/A**

Name	District	Obamacare Yes/No Vote	% of Vote Received McCain	NTU Score/ Grade
Rep. Ike Skelton	MO-4	N	60%	6% /F
Rep. Harry Teague	NM-2	N	50%	N/A**
Rep. Michael McMahon	NY-13	N	51%	N/A**
Rep. Mike McIntyre	NC-7	N	52%	29% /D
Rep. Heath Shuler	NC-52	N	52%	26% /D
Rep. Earl Pomeroy	ND-AL	Y	53%	6% /F
Rep. Charlie Wilson Jr.	OH-6	Y	50%	6% /F
Rep. John Boccieri	OH-16	Y	50%	N/A**
Rep. Zackary Space	OH-18	N	53%	5% /F
Rep. Dan Boren	OK-2	N	66%	16% /F
Rep. Kathleen Dahlkemper	PA-3	Y	49%	*N/A**
Rep. Jason Altmire	PA-4	N	55%	21% /F
Rep. Christopher Carney	PA-10	Y	53%	18% /F
Rep. Tim Holden	PA-17	N	51%	18% /F
Rep. John Spratt, Jr.	SC-5	Y	53%	6% /F
Rep. Stephanie Herseth Sandlin	SD-AL	N	53%	22% /F
Rep. Lincoln DavisT	N-4	N	64%	16% /F
Rep. Bart Gordon	TN-6	Y	62%	6% /F
Rep. John Tanner	TN-8	N	56%	5% /F
Rep. Chet Edwards	TX-17	N	67%	6% /F
Rep. Jim Matheson	UT-2	N	58%	40% /C-
Rep. Thomas Perriello	VA-5	Y	51%	N/A**
Rep. Rick Boucher	VA-9	N	59%	7% /F
Rep. Alan Mollohan	WV-1	Y	57%	6% /F
Rep. Nick Rahall, II	WV-3	Y	56%	11% /F

*Sources: Partisan Voting Index, Districts of the 111th Congress, *The Cook Political Report*; Congressional Rating Supplement, *National Taxpayer's Union*.

House Key		
Score	**Grade**	**Comments**
80% or more	A	Taxpayers' Friend
75%–79%	B+	
65%–74%	B	Good
60%–64%	B-	
55%–59%	C+	
50%–54%	C	Satisfactory
36%–49%	C-	
26%-35%	D	Poor
25% or less	F	Big Spender

*Score based on less than 75% but more than 50% of weighted total of votes cast.

**Voted on 50% or less of weighted total of votes cast, score and grade not issued.

Taxpayer Scores		
Senate		**House**
32%	Average	36%
23%	Median	22%
96%	High	98%
2%	Low	2%
	Party Scores	
8%	Democratic Average	11%
5%	Democratic Median	9%
57%	Republican Average	65%
55%	Republican Median	66%

★
Blue Dog Democrats
★

THE **"BLUE DOGS"** are a group of Democrats in the U.S. House that meet together. They consider themselves to be conservative Democrates, especially on economic issues. Decide for yourself . . . Of course, anytime they want to stand firm we'll applaud their action. Below is a listing of the Blue Dogs along with their National Taxpayer's Union scores as described in the previous section on Vulnerable Democrats.

Name	Obamacare Yes/No Vote	NTU Score/ Grade
Bright, Bobby	N	(AL-02)N/A**
Griffith, Parker	N	(AL-05)N/A**
Berry, Marion	N	(AR-01)6% /F
Ross, Mike	N	(AR-04)7%/ F
Giffords, Gabrielle	Y	(AZ-08)19% /F
Mitchell, Harry	Y	(AZ-05)31% /D
Baca, Joe	Y	(CA-43)11% /F
Cardoza, Dennis	Y	(CA-18)9% /F
Costa, Jim	Y	(CA-20)7% / F

Name	Obamacare Yes/No Vote	NTU Score/ Grade
Harman, Jane	Y	(CA-36)13% /F
Sanchez, Loretta	Y	(CA-47) 19% /F
Schiff, Adam	Y	(CA-29)13% /F
Thompson, Mike	Y	(CA-01)13% /F
Salazar, John	Y	(CO-03)14% /F
Boyd, Allen	Y	(FL-02)13% /F
Barrow, John	N	(GA-12) 28% /D
Bishop, Sanford	Y	(GA-02)5% /F
Marshall, Jim	N	(GA-03)22% /F
Scott, David	Y	(GA-13)9% /F
Boswell, Leonard	Y	(IA-03)6% /F
Minnick, Walt	N	(ID-01)N/A**
Donnelly, Joe	Y	(IN-02) 16% /F
Ellsworth, Brad	Y	(IN-08)15% /F
Hill, Baron	Y	(IN-09)22% /F
Moore, Dennis	Y	(KS-03)6% /F
Chandler, Ben	N	(KY-06)15% /F
Melancon, Charlie	N	(LA-03)8% /F
Kratovil, Jr., Frank	N	(MD-01)N/A**
Michaud, Mike	Y	(ME-02)20% /F
Peterson, Collin	N	(MN-07)21% /F
Childers, Travis	N	(MS-01)31% /D
Taylor, Gene	N	(MS-04)20% /F
McIntyre, Mike	N	(NC-07)29% /D
Shuler, Heath	N	(NC-11)26% /D
Pomeroy, Earl	N	(ND)6% /F
Arcuri, Mike	N	(NY-24)8% /F

Name	Obamacare Yes/No Vote	NTU Score/ Grade
Space, Zack	N	(OH-18)5% /F
Wilson, Charles	Y	(OH-06)6% /F
Boren, Dan	N	(OK-02)16% /F
Altmire, Jason	N	(PA-04) 21% /F
Carney, Christopher	Y	(PA-10)18% /F
Dahlkemper, Kathy	Y	(PA-03)N/A**
Holden, Tim	N	(PA-17)18% /F
Murphy, Patrick	Y	(PA-08)12% /F
Herseth Sandlin, Stephanie	N	(SD)22% /F
Cooper, Jim	Y	(TN-05) 26% /D
Davis, Lincoln	N	(TN-04) 16% /F
Gordon, Bart	Y	(TN-06)6% /F
Tanner, John	N	(TN-08)5% /F
Cuellar, Henry	Y	(TX-28) 14% /F
Matheson, Jim	N	(UT-02) 40% /C-
Nye, Glenn	N	(VA-02) N/A**

**footnote: Source: Congressional Rating Supplement, *National Taxpayer's Union.*

★ National Resources ★

LISTED BELOW are just a few websites where you can obtain information on what is happening in your government, and find factual information to share with friends.

Roll Call (Congress.org)
★ ★ ★

ROLL CALL is the foremost Capitol Hill publication with the largest readership among Congressional decision makers. Go to their website, put in your zip code and you will find the elected officials that represent the area where yours live. Sometimes Congressional or state districts will have only a portion of a zip code area. In that case you must put in your full 9 digit zip code or home address. You will be given a listing of your two US Senators, your Congressman, the governor of your state, and your state senator and state representative. Next you can click on each of their names to obtain their contact information, and other relative information about them such as their committee assignments. **You may request notification of any federal representative or senator's vote on any piece of legislation, and receive this information by email weekly.**

Newt.org
★ ★ ★

THE OFFICIAL WEBSITE of former Speaker of the House Newt Gingrich. This website has a wealth of information on a number of subjects. You can also sign up to get frequent updates on subjects of interest to conservative voters and consumers. Newt is the author of several very interesting and informative books, both fiction and nonfiction, and you can read about these on the website. You can also order his books, audiotapes, and video items directly from the website.

Center for Health Transformation
★ ★ ★

1425 K Street, NW
Suite 450
Washington, DC 20005
(202) 375-2001

5555 Glenridge Connector
Suite 425
Atlanta, GA 30342
(404) 201-7909

111 Westport Plaza
Suite 600
St. Louis, MO 63146
(314) 542 3022

info@healthtransformation.net
The email address is the same for all three offices.

The Center for Health Transformation is a high-impact collaboration of private and public sector leaders committed to creating a 21st Century Intelligent Health System that saves lives and saves money for all Americans. It was founded and is lead by Newt Gingrich.

The Center is based on the following premise: Small changes or reactionary fixes to separate pieces of the current system have not and will not work. We need a system-wide transformation. Unlike other alliances, the Center unites stakeholders across the spectrum (providers, employers, vendors, trade associations, disease groups, think tanks) and government leaders at both the state and federal level to drive transformation according to a shared vision and key principles.

Rush Limbaugh
★★★

You can call The Rush Limbaugh Show program line between 12 Noon and 3PM Eastern Time at: 1-800-282-2882
You can e-mail Rush at: ElRushbo@eibnet.com
You can fax Rush at: 212-445-3963
You can write Rush at:

> The Rush Limbaugh Show
> 1270 Avenue of the Americas
> New York, NY 10020

Fox News.com
★★★

This is the **ONLY** cable network for conservatives. On Fox's home page you can leave an email for Hannity, O'Reilly, Glenn Beck, or any of the other commentators. You can also simply type the name of the program or personality to find out how to contact them. An example would be Hannity@FoxNews.com to get Sean Hannity. Also, see phone numbers, etc. listed in the section on TV Networks & Washington DC Stations.

Small Business & Entrepreneurship Council (SBE Council)
★★★

> 2944 Hunter Mill Road, Suite 204
> Oakton, VA 22124
> Phone: (703) 242-5840
> Fax: (703) 242-5841
> Email: membership@sbecouncil.org

The Small Business and Entrepreneurship Council (SBE Council) works to educate elected officials, policy makers, business leaders and the public about initiatives that enhance the environment for entrepreneurship, business start-up and growth through advocacy, research, training and education, *SBE Council members and staff convey the importance of entrepreneurship and small business to job creation, innovation and the overall health of the economy. The SBE Council is viewed as one of the most powerful and effective organizations dedicated to protecting small business and promoting entrepreneurship.*

National Taxpayers Union
★ ★ ★

108 N. Alfred St.
Alexandria, VA 22314
Phone: (703) 683-5700
Email NTU@NTU.ORG

This group is a nonprofit citizens' organization working for lower taxes, less wasteful spending and accountability for all levels of government. They also produce a scorecard that rates the votes of federal officials on important economic and tax issues, according to whether their vote will add or subtract from the tax burden on the taxpayer.

Citizens for a Sound Economy
★ ★ ★

1523 16th Street, NW, 2nd Floor
Washington, DC 20036
Phone: (202) 783-3870
Fax: (202) 232-8356
Toll Free: 1-888-564-6273
E-mail: cse@cse.org
http://www.cse.org

CSE is a conservative public policy organization.

American Legislative Exchange Council (ALEC)
★★★

1101 Vermont Ave., NW, 11th Floor
Washington, D.C. 20005
Phone: 202-466-3800 | Fax: 202-466-3801
Website: alec.org

ALEC is an organization for conservative state legislators and business leaders working to support and develop new issues at the state level. It produces model legislation and develops reports comparing one state to another.

Americans For Prosperity
★★★

2111 Wilson Blvd. Suite 350
Arlington, VA 22201
Phone: (703) 224-3200
Toll Free: (866) 730-0150
americansforposperity.org

A group dedicated to educating citizens on economic policy and mobilizing those citzens as advocates in the public policy ares most states have chapters

Tax Foundation
★★★

National Press Building
529 14th Street, NW
Suite 420
Washington, D.C. 20045-1000
(Phone) 202.464.6200
Email: tf@taxfoundation.org

The Tax Foundation is a sixty-five year old nonpartisan group that wants to make Americans more aware of the impact of the tax burden.

Heritage Foundation
———★★★———

214 Massachusetts Ave NE
Washington D.C. 20002-4999
Phone 202.546.4400
Fax 202.546.8328

The Heritage Foundation is a Washington based conservative think tank, that provide invaluable resources to various groups. Their stated goal is, "To formulate and promote conservative public policies based on the principles of free enterprise, limited government, individual freedom, traditional American values, and a strong national defense."

Americans for Tax Reform
———★★★———

722 12th Street NW, Suite 400
Washington, D.C. 20005
Office 202-785-0266
Fax 202-785-0261
Website: friends@atr.org

The most constant anti-tax increase organization in America

American Enterprise Institute for Public Policy Research
———★★★———

1150 Seventeenth Street, N.W.
Washington, D.C. 20036
Phone: 202-862-5800
Main fax: 202-862-7177
Questions or comments about the website:
Webmaster@aei.org

After seven decades, AEI continues to serve a vital role in the intellectual life of the nation. The Institute furnishes policymakers with ideas to meet the pressing challenges of today based on the resilient principles of private liberty, individual opportunity, and free enterprise.

The 60 Plus Association
———★★★———

The 60 Plus Association
515 King Street   Suite 315
Alexandria, Virginia 22314
Phone (703) 807-2070
Fax (703) 807-2073
info@60plus.org

This is the conservatives answer to AARP. The association believes in free enterprise, less government, lower taxes approach to seniors issues.

Betsy McCaughey
———★★★———

212-360-6524
defendyourhealthcare.us

The Honorable Betsy McCaughey is a former Lt. Governor of New York state and has written a number of articles on the current healthcare debate and other health care issues.

TV NETWORKS & WASHINGTON, DC STATIONS
———★★★———

NOTE ON MEDIA COMPLAINTS: When you are displeased with the media, it is usually more effective to contact the sponsors of a given program than to speak directly to the media outlet. A sponsor who threatens to withdraw their financial support due to a public outrage is a larger concern than a lost viewer. Most sponsors do not want their name associated with controversial issues.

Fox News Channel
1211 Avenue of the Americas
New York, NY 10036
Phone (212) 301-3000
Fax (212) 301-4229
Comments@FoxNews.com

Satellite Radio
———★ ★ ★———

There are two networks, Sirius and XM that have now merged, but they still are accessed separately. The first four channels are conservative and the last two are liberal, left wing channels included for your comic relief.

	Sirius	XM
Fox News	131	121
Patriot Channel	144	138
America Right	161	66
Fox News Talk	145	168
Left Channel	146	137
America Left	17	167

ABC
77 West 66th St.
New York, NY 10023
Phone (212) 456-7777
netaudr@abc.com

CBS News
524 West 57th Street
New York, NY 10019
Phone (212) 975-4321
Fax (212) 975-1893

NBC
30 Rockefeller Plaza
New York, NY 10112
Phone (212) 664-4444
Fax (212) 664-4426
Go to NBC.com and choose category of program.

News Hour with Jim Lehrer

3620 S. 27th Street

Arlington, VA 22206

Phone (703) 998-2150

Newshour@pbs.org

CNBC

2700 Fletcher Ave.

Fort Lee, NJ 07024

Phone (201) 585-2622

Fax (201) 583-5453

Info@cnbc.com

CNN

ONE CNN Center

Box 105336

Atlanta, GA 30303-5366

Phone (404) 827-2600

CNN.feedback@CNN.Com

MSNBC

ONE MSNBC Plaza

Secaucus, NJ 07094

Phone (201) 583-5000

Fax (201) 583-5453

world@msnbc.com

PBS

1320 Braddock Place

Alexandria, VA 22314

Phone (703) 739-5000

Fax (703) 739-8458

NPR

635 Massachusetts Ave NW
Washington, DC 20001-3753
Phone (202) 513-2000
Fax (202) 513-3329
Ombudsman@NPR.ORG

WETA Channel 26

2775 S. Quincy St.
Arlington, VA 22206
Phone (703) 998-2600

WRC (NBC-DC)

4001 Nebraska Ave. NW
Washington, DC 20016
Phone (202) 885-4000
Fax (202) 885-5022

Whether elected or appointed
He considers himself the Lord's anointed
And indeed the ointment lingers on him
So thick you can't get your fingers on him.
—Ogden Nash

★ HOUSE MEMBERS ★

Member Name	District	State	DC Phone	DC FAX	Email
Rep. Jo Bonner (R)	1	Alabama	202-225-4931	202-225-0562	http://bonner.house.gov/HoR/AL01/Contact+Jo/Email+Jo/
Rep. Bobby Bright (D)	2	Alabama	202-225-2901	202-225-8913	https://forms.house.gov/bright/contact-form.shtml
Rep. Mike Rogers (R)	3	Alabama	202-225-3261	202-226-8485	http://www.house.gov/mike-rogers/contact.shtml
Rep. Robert B. Aderholt (R)	4	Alabama	202-225-4876	202-225-5587	http://aderholt.house.gov/?sectionid=195&sectiontree=195
Rep. Parker Griffith (D)	5	Alabama	202-225-4801	202-225-4392	https://forms.house.gov/griffith/contact-form.shtml
Rep. Spencer Bachus (R)	6	Alabama	202-225-4921	202-225-2082	http://www.house.gov/writerep/
Rep. Artur Davis (D)	7	Alabama	202-225-2665	202-226-9567	http://arturdavis.house.gov/index.cfm?p=ContactCongressmanDavis
Rep. Don Young (R)	At Large	Alaska	202-225-5765	202-225-0425	http://donyoung.house.gov/IMA/issue_subscribe.htm
Del. Eni F. H. Faleomavaega (D)	At Large	American Samoa	202-225-8577	202-225-8757	faleomavaega@mail.house.gov
Rep. Ann Kirkpatrick (D)	1	Arizona	202-225-2315	202-226-9739	https://forms.house.gov/kirkpatrick/contact-form.shtml
Rep. Trent Franks (R)	2	Arizona	202-225-4576	202-225-6328	http://www.house.gov/franks/IMA/email.shtml
Rep. John Shadegg (R)	3	Arizona	202-225-3361	202-225-3462	http://johnshadegg.house.gov/Contact/ContactForm.htm
Rep. Ed Pastor (D)	4	Arizona	202-225-4065	202-225-1655	http://www.house.gov/writerep/
Rep. Harry Mitchell (D)	5	Arizona	202-225-2190	202-225-3263	https://forms.house.gov/mitchell/webforms/issue_subscribe.htm
Rep. Jeff Flake (R)	6	Arizona	202-225-2635	202-226-4386	http://www.house.gov/writerep/
Rep. Raul Grijalva (D)	7	Arizona	202-225-2435	202-225-1541	http://grijalva.house.gov/?sectionid=498&sectiontree=249
Rep. Gabrielle Giffords (D)	8	Arizona	202-225-2542	202-225-0378	https://giffordsforms.house.gov/contact/email.shtml
Rep. Marion Berry (D)	1	Arkansas	202-225-4076	202-225-5602	http://www.house.gov/berry/zipauth.shtml
Rep. Vic Snyder (D)	2	Arkansas	202-225-2506	202-225-5903	http://www.house.gov/snyder/contact-form.shtml

Member Name	District	State	DC Phone	DC FAX	Email
Rep. John Boozman (R)	3	Arkansas	202-225-4301	202-225-5713	http://www.house.gov/writerep/
Rep. Mike Ross (D)	4	Arkansas	202-225-3772	202-225-1314	http://ross.house.gov/?sectionid=77&sectiontree=7677
Rep. Mike Thompson (D)	1	California	202-225-3311	202-225-4335	http://mikethompson.house.gov/contact/email.shtml
Rep. Wally Herger (R)	2	California	202-225-3076	202-226-0852	https://forms.house.gov/herger/webforms/landing.html
Rep. Dan Lungren (R)	3	California	202-225-5716	202-226-1298	http://lungren.house.gov/index.php?option=com_content&
Rep. Tom McClintock (R)	4	California	202-225-2511	202-225-5444	https://forms.house.gov/mcclintock/contact-form.shtml
Rep. Doris Matsui (D)	5	California	202-225-7163	202-225-0566	https://forms.house.gov/matsui/webforms/issue_subscribe.htm
Rep. Lynn Woolsey (D)	6	California	202-225-5161	202-225-5163	http://woolsey.house.gov/contactemailform.asp
Rep. George Miller (D)	7	California	202-225-2095	202-225-5609	http://georgemiller.house.gov/contactus/2007/08/post_1.html
Rep. Nancy Pelosi (D)	8	California	202-225-4965	202-225-4188	sf.nancy@mail.house.gov
Rep. Barbara Lee (D)	9	California	202-225-2661	202-225-9817	http://lee.house.gov/?sectionid=128&sectiontree=18128
Rep. Jerry McNerney (D)	11	California	202-225-1947	202-225-4060	http://mcnerney.house.gov/contact.shtml
Rep. Jackie Speier (D)	12	California	202-225-3531	202-226-4183	http://speier.house.gov/index.cfm?sectionid=54&sectiontree=54
Rep. Pete Stark (D)	13	California	202-225-5065	202-226-3805	https://forms.house.gov/stark/webforms/contact.htm
Rep. Anna G. Eshoo (D)	14	California	202-225-8104	202-225-8890	https://forms.house.gov/eshoo/webforms/issue_subscribe.htm
Rep. Mike Honda (D)	15	California	202-225-2631	202-225-2699	http://www.honda.house.gov/contactmike.shtml
Rep. Zoe Lofgren (D)	16	California	202-225-3072	202-225-3336	http://forms.house.gov/lofgren/webforms/contactzipauth.html
Rep. Sam Farr (D)	17	California	202-225-2861	202-225-6791	http://www.farr.house.gov/index.php?
Rep. Dennis Cardoza (D)	18	California	202-225-6131	202-225-0819	http://www.house.gov/writerep/
Rep. George Radanovich (R)	19	California	202-225-4540	202-225-3402	http://radanovich.house.gov/Contact/email.htm

Member Name	District	State	DC Phone	DC FAX	Email
Rep. Jim Costa (D)	20	California	202-225-3341	202-225-9308	http://www.house.gov/formcosta/issue.htm
Rep. Devin Nunes (R)	21	California	202-225-2523	202-225-3404	http://www.nunes.house.gov/index.cfm?FuseAction=ContactUs.ContactForm
Rep. Kevin McCarthy (R)	22	California	202-225-2915	202-225-2908	https://kevinmccarthyforms.house.gov/showpage.asp?ID=69
Rep. Lois Capps (D)	23	California	202-225-3601	202-225-5632	http://www.house.gov/capps/contact/send_an_email.shtml
Rep. Elton Gallegly (R)	24	California	202-225-5811	202-225-1100	http://www.house.gov/writerep/
Rep. Howard P. (Buck) McKeon (R)	25	California	202-225-1956	202-226-0683	http://mckeon.house.gov/contact.shtml
Rep. David Dreier (R)	26	California	202-225-2305	202-225-7018	http://dreier.house.gov/contact.shtml
Rep. Brad Sherman (D)	27	California	202-225-5911	202-225-5879	http://www.house.gov/sherman/contact/
Rep. Howard L. Berman (D)	28	California	202-225-4695	202-225-3196	http://www.house.gov/berman/contact/
Rep. Adam Schiff (D)	29	California	202-225-4176	202-225-5828	http://schiff.house.gov/HoR/CA29/Contact+Information/Contact+Form.htm
Rep. Henry A. Waxman (D)	30	California	202-225-3976	202-225-4099	http://waxman.house.gov/Contact/
Rep. Xavier Becerra (D)	31	California	202-225-6235	202-225-2202	http://becerra.house.gov/HoR/CA31/Hidden+Content/Email+Signup+Form.htm
Rep. Diane Watson (D)	33	California	202-225-7084	202-225-2422	http://www.house.gov/watson/zipauth.shtml
Rep. Lucille Roybal-Allard (D)	34	California	202-225-1766	202-226-0350	http://roybal-allard.house.gov/Contact/
Rep. Maxine Waters (D)	35	California	202-225-2201	202-225-7854	http://www.house.gov/waters/IMA/issue.htm
Rep. Jane Harman (D)	36	California	202-225-8220	202-226-7290	http://www.house.gov/harman/contact/email.shtml
Rep. Laura Richardson (D)	37	California	202-225-7924	202-225-7926	http://richardson.house.gov/IMA/issue_subscribe.htm
Rep. Grace Napolitano (D)	38	California	202-225-5256	202-225-0027	http://www.napolitano.house.gov/contact/feedback.htm
Rep. Linda Sanchez (D)	39	California	202-225-6676	202-226-1012	http://www.lindasanchez.house.gov/index.cfm?section=contact
Rep. Ed Royce (R)	40	California	202-225-4111	202-226-0335	http://www.house.gov/writerep/

Member Name	District	State	DC Phone	DC FAX	Email
Rep. Jerry Lewis (R)	41	California	202-225-5861	202-225-6498	http://www.house.gov/jerrylewis/WritetoRepresentativeLewis.htm
Rep. Gary Miller (R)	42	California	202-225-3201	202-226-6962	http://garymiller.house.gov/Contact/
Rep. Joe Baca (D)	43	California	202-225-6161	202-225-8671	http://www.house.gov/writerep/
Rep. Ken Calvert (R)	44	California	202-225-1986	202-225-2004	http://calvert.house.gov/xcvwe3.asp
Rep. Mary Bono Mack (R)	45	California	202-225-5330	202-225-2961	http://bono.house.gov/Contact_Mary/ContactForm.htm
Rep. Dana Rohrabacher (R)	46	California	202-225-2415	202-225-0145	http://www.house.gov/writerep/
Rep. Loretta Sanchez (D)	47	California	202-225-2965	202-225-5859	http://www.lorettasanchez.house.gov/forms/contact.html
Rep. John Campbell (R)	48	California	202-225-5611	202-225-9177	https://forms.house.gov/campbell/webforms/issue_subscribe.htm
Rep. Darrell Issa (R)	49	California	202-225-3906	202-225-3303	http://issa.house.gov/index.cfm?FuseAction=Contact.ContactForm
Rep. Brian Bilbray (R)	50	California	202-225-0508	202-225-2558	http://www.house.gov/bilbray/contact.shtml
Rep. Bob Filner (D)	51	California	202-225-8045	202-225-9073	http://www.house.gov/writerep/
Rep. Duncan D. Hunter (R)	52	California	202-225-5672	202-225-0235	https://forms.house.gov/hunter/contact-form.shtml
Rep. Susan Davis (D)	53	California	202-225-2040	202-225-2948	http://www.house.gov/susandavis/contact.shtml
Rep. Diana DeGette (D)	1	Colorado	202-225-4431	202-225-5657	http://www.house.gov/formdegette/zip_auth.htm
Rep. Jared Polis (D)	2	Colorado	202-225-2161	202-226-7840	http://polis.house.gov/Contact/
Rep. John Salazar (D)	3	Colorado	202-225-4761	202-226-9669	http://www.house.gov/salazar/contact.shtml
Rep. Betsy Markey (D)	4	Colorado	202-225-4676	202-225-5870	http://betsymarkey.house.gov/Contact/
Rep. Doug Lamborn (R)	5	Colorado	202-225-4422	202-226-2638	http://lamborn.house.gov/index.cfm?sectionid=64&sectiontree=364
Rep. Mike Coffman (R)	6	Colorado	202-225-7882	202-226-4623	https://forms.house.gov/coffman/contact-form.shtml
Rep. Ed Perlmutter (D)	7	Colorado	202-225-2645	202-225-5278	http://perlmutter.house.gov/IMA/issue_subscribe.htm

Member Name	District	State	DC Phone	DC FAX	Email
Rep. John Larson (D)	1	Connecticut	202-225-2265	202-225-1031	http://forms.house.gov/larson/contact.html
Rep. Joe Courtney (D)	2	Connecticut	202-225-2076	202-225-4977	http://courtney.house.gov/email/
Rep. Rosa L. DeLauro (D)	3	Connecticut	202-225-3661	202-225-4890	http://delauro.house.gov/contact_form_email.cfm
Rep. Jim Himes (D)	4	Connecticut	202-225-5541	202-225-9629	http://himes.house.gov/?sectionid=54&sectiontree=54
Rep. Chris Murphy (D)	5	Connecticut	202-225-4476	202-225-5933	http://www.house.gov/formchrismurphy/ic_zip_auth.htm
Rep. Mike Castle (R)	At Large	Delaware	202-225-4165	202-225-2291	http://www.castle.house.gov/Contact/
Del. Eleanor Holmes Norton (D)	At Large	District of Columbia	202-225-8050	202-225-3002	http://www.norton.house.gov/forms/contact.html
Rep. Jeff Miller (R)	1	Florida	202-225-4136	202-225-3414	http://jeffmiller.house.gov/index.cfm?FuseAction=Contact.Home
Rep. Allen Boyd (D)	2	Florida	202-225-5235	202-225-5615	http://www.house.gov/boyd/zip_authen.html
Rep. Corrine Brown (D)	3	Florida	202-225-0123	202-225-2256	http://www.house.gov/corrinebrown/IMA/issue.shtml
Rep. Ander Crenshaw (R)	4	Florida	202-225-2501	202-225-2504	http://www.house.gov/writerep/
Rep. Ginny Brown-Waite (R)	5	Florida	202-225-1002	202-226-6559	http://www.house.gov/formbrown-waite/IMA/issue_subscribe.htm
Rep. Cliff Stearns (R)	6	Florida	202-225-5744	202-225-3973	http://www.house.gov/writerep/
Rep. John L. Mica (R)	7	Florida	202-225-4035	202-226-0821	http://www.house.gov/mica/messageform.shtml
Rep. Alan Grayson (D)	8	Florida	202-225-2176	202-225-0999	https://forms.house.gov/grayson/contact-form.shtml
Rep. Gus Bilirakis (R)	9	Florida	202-225-5755	202-225-4085	http://www.house.gov/formbilirakis/issue_subscribe.htm
Rep. C. W. (Bill) Young (R)	10	Florida	202-225-5961	202-225-9764	Bill.Young@mail.house.gov
Rep. Kathy Anne Castor (D)	11	Florida	202-225-3376	202-225-5652	http://www.house.gov/writerep/
Rep. Adam Putnam (R)	12	Florida	202-225-1252	202-226-0585	http://adamputnam.house.gov/contact.shtml
Rep. Vern Buchanan (R)	13	Florida	202-225-5015	202-226-0828	http://buchanan.house.gov/contact.shtml

Member Name	District	State	DC Phone	DC FAX	Email
Rep. Connie Mack (R)	14	Florida	202-225-2536	202-226-0439	https://mack.house.gov/?p=Email
Rep. Bill Posey (R)	15	Florida	202-225-3671	202-225-3516	http://posey.house.gov/Contact/
Rep. Tom Rooney (R)	16	Florida	202-225-5792	202-225-3132	https://forms.house.gov/rooney/contact-form.shtml
Rep. Kendrick B. Meek (D)	17	Florida	202-225-4506	202-226-0777	http://kendrickmeek.house.gov/contact1.shtml
Rep. Ileana Ros-Lehtinen (R)	18	Florida	202-225-3931	202-225-5620	http://www.house.gov/writerep/
Rep. Robert Wexler (D)	19	Florida	202-225-3001	202-225-5974	http://www.wexler.house.gov/email.shtml
Rep. Debbie Wasserman Schultz (D)	20	Florida	202-225-7931	202-226-2052	http://wassermanschultz.house.gov/zipauth.htm
Rep. Lincoln Diaz-Balart (R)	21	Florida	202-225-4211	202-225-8576	http://diaz-balart.house.gov/index.cfm?FuseAction=Offices.Contact
Rep. Ron Klein (D)	22	Florida	202-225-3026	202-225-8398	http://klein.house.gov/?sectionid=4&sectiontree=4
Rep. Alcee L. Hastings (D)	23	Florida	202-225-1313	202-225-1171	https://forms.house.gov/alceehastings/webforms/issue_subscribe.htm
Rep. Suzanne Kosmas (D)	24	Florida	202-225-2706	202-226-6299	https://forms.house.gov/kosmas/contact-form.shtml
Rep. Mario Diaz-Balart (R)	25	Florida	202-225-2778	202-226-0346	http://www.house.gov/formmariodiaz-balart/ic_zip_auth.htm
Rep. Jack Kingston (R)	1	Georgia	202-225-5831	202-226-2269	http://kingston.house.gov/ContactForm/zipauth.htm
Rep. Sanford D. Bishop, Jr. (D)	2	Georgia	202-225-3631	202-225-2203	http://bishop.house.gov/display.cfm?content_id=229
Rep. Lynn Westmoreland (R)	3	Georgia	202-225-5901	202-225-2515	http://www.house.gov/writerep/
Rep. Hank Johnson (D)	4	Georgia	202-225-1605	202-226-0691	http://hankjohnson.house.gov/contact_hank_write.shtml
Rep. John Lewis (D)	5	Georgia	202-225-3801	202-225-0351	http://www.house.gov/formjohnlewis/contact.html
Rep. Tom Price (R)	6	Georgia	202-225-4501	202-225-4656	http://tomprice.house.gov/html/contact_form_email.cfm
Rep. John Linder (R)	7	Georgia	202-225-4272	202-225-4696	http://linder.house.gov/index.cfm?FuseAction=ContactJohn.ContactForm
Rep. Jim Marshall (D)	8	Georgia	202-225-6531	202-225-3013	http://www.house.gov/writerep/

Member Name	District	State	DC Phone	DC FAX	Email
Rep. Nathan Deal (R)	9	Georgia	202-225-5211	202-225-8272	http://www.house.gov/deal/contact.shtml
Rep. Paul C. Broun (R)	10	Georgia	202-225-4101	202-226-0776	http://broun.house.gov/Contact/zipauth.htm
Rep. Phil Gingrey (R)	11	Georgia	202-225-2931	202-225-2944	http://www.house.gov/formgingrey/IMA/issue.htm
Rep. John Barrow (D)	12	Georgia	202-225-2823	202-225-3377	https://forms.house.gov/barrow/webforms/issue_subscribe.htm
Rep. David Scott (D)	13	Georgia	202-225-2939	202-225-4628	http://www.house.gov/writerep/
Del. Madeleine Bordallo (D)	At Large	Guam	202-225-1188	202-226-0341	http://www.house.gov/bordallo/IMA/issue.htm
Rep. Neil Abercrombie (D)	1	Hawaii	202-225-2726	202-225-4580	http://www.house.gov/abercrombie/e_form.shtml
Rep. Mazie Hirono (D)	2	Hawaii	202-225-4906	202-225-4987	http://hirono.house.gov/IMA/issue_subscribe.htm
Rep. Walter C. (Walt) Minnick (D)	1	Idaho	202-225-6611	202-225-3029	https://forms.house.gov/minnick/contact-form.shtml
Rep. Mike Simpson (R)	2	Idaho	202-225-5531	202-225-8216	http://www.house.gov/simpson/emailme.shtml
Rep. Bobby L. Rush (D)	1	Illinois	202-225-4372	202-226-0333	http://www.house.gov/rush/zipauth.shtml
Rep. Jesse L. Jackson, Jr. (D)	2	Illinois	202-225-0773	202-225-0899	http://www.jessejacksonjr.org/contact.htm
Rep. Dan Lipinski (D)	3	Illinois	202-225-5701	202-225-1012	http://www.house.gov/formlipinski/zipauth.html
Rep. Luis V. Gutierrez (D)	4	Illinois	202-225-8203	202-225-7810	http://luisgutierrez.house.gov/singlepage.aspx?newsid=1262
Rep. Mike Quigley (D)	5	Illinois	202-225-4061	202-225-5603	https://forms.house.gov/quigley/contact-form.shtml
Rep. Peter Roskam (R)	6	Illinois	202-225-4561	202-225-1166	http://www.house.gov/writerep/
Rep. Danny Davis (D)	7	Illinois	202-225-5006	202-225-5641	https://forms.house.gov/davis/webforms/issue_subscribe.htm
Rep. Melissa Bean (D)	8	Illinois	202-225-3711	202-225-7830	http://www.house.gov/bean/issue_subscribe.htm
Rep. Janice Schakowsky (D)	9	Illinois	202-225-2111	202-226-6890	http://www.house.gov/schakowsky/email.shtml
Rep. Mark Steven Kirk (R)	10	Illinois	202-225-4835	202-225-0837	http://www.house.gov/kirk/zipauth.shtml

Member Name	District	State	DC Phone	DC FAX	Email
Rep. Debbie Halvorson (D)	11	Illinois	202-225-3635	202-225-3521	https://forms.house.gov/halvorson/contact-form.shtml
Rep. Jerry F. Costello (D)	12	Illinois	202-225-5661	202-225-0285	http://costello.house.gov/IMA/issue_subscribe.shtml
Rep. Judy Biggert (R)	13	Illinois	202-225-3515	202-225-9420	http://judybiggert.house.gov/ContactJudy.aspx
Rep. Bill Foster (D)	14	Illinois	202-225-2976	202-225-0697	http://foster.house.gov/Contact/
Rep. Timothy V. Johnson (R)	15	Illinois	202-225-2371	202-226-0791	http://timjohnson.house.gov/?sectionid=56&sectiontree=356
Rep. Don Manzullo (R)	16	Illinois	202-225-5676	202-225-5284	http://manzullo.house.gov/zipauth.aspx
Rep. Phil Hare (D)	17	Illinois	202-225-5905	202-225-5396	http://hare.house.gov/?sectionid=74&sectiontree=445074
Rep. Aaron Schock (R)	18	Illinois	202-225-6201	202-225-9249	https://forms.house.gov/schock/contact-form.shtml
Rep. John Shimkus (R)	19	Illinois	202-225-5271	202-225-5880	http://shimkus.house.gov/?sectionid=54&sectiontree=5154
Rep. Peter J. Visclosky (D)	1	Indiana	202-225-2461	202-225-2493	http://www.house.gov/writerep/
Rep. Joe Donnelly (D)	2	Indiana	202-225-3915	202-225-6798	http://donnelly.house.gov/issue_subscribe.shtml
Rep. Mark Souder (R)	3	Indiana	202-225-4436	202-225-3479	http://souder.house.gov/index.cfm?FuseAction=Contact.ContactForm
Rep. Steve Buyer (R)	4	Indiana	202-225-5037	202-225-2267	http://www.house.gov/writerep/
Rep. Dan Burton (R)	5	Indiana	202-225-2276	202-225-0016	http://burton.house.gov/contacts/add/type:contact
Rep. Mike Pence (R)	6	Indiana	202-225-3021	202-225-3382	https://forms.house.gov/pence/IMA/contact_form.htm
Rep. Andre Carson (D)	7	Indiana	202-225-4011	202-225-5633	http://forms.house.gov/carson/webforms/issue_subscribe.htm
Rep. Brad Ellsworth (D)	8	Indiana	202-225-4636	202-225-3284	http://www.ellsworth.house.gov/index.php?
Rep. Baron Hill (D)	9	Indiana	202-225-5315	202-226-6866	http://baronhill.house.gov/IMA/issue_subscribe.shtml
Rep. Bruce Braley (D)	1	Iowa	202-225-2911	202-225-6666	https://forms.house.gov/braley/webforms/issue_subscribe.html
Rep. Dave Loebsack (D)	2	Iowa	202-225-6576	202-226-0757	http://loebsack.house.gov/contactform/

Member Name	District	State	DC Phone	DC FAX	Email
Rep. Leonard L. Boswell (D)	3	Iowa	202-225-3806	202-225-5608	http://boswell.house.gov/?sectionid=81&sectiontree=481
Rep. Tom Latham (R)	4	Iowa	202-225-5476	202-225-3301	http://www.tomlatham.house.gov/Contact/
Rep. Steve King (R)	5	Iowa	202-225-4426	202-225-3193	http://steveking.house.gov/index.cfm?FuseAction=ContactUs.ContactForm
Rep. Jerry Moran (R)	1	Kansas	202-225-2715	202-225-5124	http://www.jerrymoran.house.gov/index.php?
Rep. Lynn Jenkins (R)	2	Kansas	202-225-6601	202-225-7986	https://forms.house.gov/lynnjenkins/contact-form.shtml
Rep. Dennis Moore (D)	3	Kansas	202-225-2865	202-225-2807	http://www.moore.house.gov/contact/index.shtml
Rep. Todd Tiahrt (R)	4	Kansas	202-225-6216	202-225-3489	http://tiahrt.house.gov/?sectionid=12
Rep. Edward Whitfield (R)	1	Kentucky	202-225-3115	202-225-3547	http://whitfield.house.gov/contact/index.shtml
Rep. Brett Guthrie (R)	2	Kentucky	202-225-3501	202-226-2019	https://forms.house.gov/guthrie/contact-form.shtml
Rep. John Yarmuth (D)	3	Kentucky	202-225-5401	202-225-5776	http://yarmuth.house.gov/?sectionid=68&sectiontree=62968
Rep. Geoff Davis (R)	4	Kentucky	202-225-3465	202-225-0003	http://geoffdavis.house.gov/Contact/
Rep. Harold Rogers (R)	5	Kentucky	202-225-4601	202-225-0940	http://halrogers.house.gov/Contact.aspx
Rep. Ben Chandler (D)	6	Kentucky	202-225-4706	202-225-2122	http://www.house.gov/writerep/
Rep. Steve Scalise (R)	1	Louisiana	202-225-3015	202-226-0386	http://www.scalise.house.gov/contactform_zipcheck.shtml
Rep. Joseph Cao (R)	2	Louisiana	202-225-6636	202-225-1988	http://josephcao.house.gov/Contact/
Rep. Charlie Melancon (D)	3	Louisiana	202-225-4031	202-226-3944	http://www.melancon.house.gov/index.php?
Rep. John Fleming (R)	4	Louisiana	202-225-2777	202-225-8039	http://fleming.house.gov/?sectionid=7&sectiontree=47
Rep. Rodney Alexander (R)	5	Louisiana	202-225-8490	202-225-5639	http://alexander.house.gov/?sectionid=7&sectiontree=47
Rep. Bill Cassidy (R)	6	Louisiana	202-225-3901	202-225-7313	https://forms.house.gov/cassidy/contact-form.shtml
Rep. Charles W. Boustany, Jr. (R)	7	Louisiana	202-225-2031	202-225-5724	http://boustany.house.gov/?sectionid=4&sectiontree=4

Member Name	District	State	DC Phone	DC FAX	Email
Rep. Chellie Pingree (D)	1	Maine	202-225-6116	202-225-5590	https://forms.house.gov/pingree/contact-form.shtml
Rep. Mike Michaud (D)	2	Maine	202-225-6306	202-225-2943	http://www.michaud.house.gov/article.asp?id=389
Rep. Frank M. Kratovil, Jr. (D)	1	Maryland	202-225-5311	202-225-0254	https://forms.house.gov/kratovil/contact-form.shtml
Rep. C. A. Dutch Ruppersberger (D)	2	Maryland	202-225-3061	202-225-3094	http://dutch.house.gov/writedutch_za.shtml
Rep. John Sarbanes (D)	3	Maryland	202-225-4016	202-225-9219	http://sarbanes.house.gov/federal.asp
Rep. Donna Edwards (D)	4	Maryland	202-225-8699	202-225-8714	http://donnaedwards.house.gov/?sectionid=52&sectiontree=452
Rep. Steny Hoyer (D)	5	Maryland2	02-225-4131	202-225-4300	http://hoyer.house.gov/contact/email.asp
Rep. Roscoe Bartlett (R)	6	Maryland	202-225-2721	202-225-2193	http://bartlett.house.gov/Email_Roscoe/
Rep. Elijah E. Cummings (D)	7	Maryland	202-225-4741	202-225-3178	http://www.house.gov/writerep/
Rep. Chris Van Hollen, Jr. (D)	8	Maryland	202-225-5341	202-225-0375	http://vanhollen.house.gov/HoR/MD08/
Rep. John W. Olver (D)	1	Massachusetts	202-225-5335	202-226-1224	http://www.house.gov/olver/contactme.html
Rep. Richard E. Neal (D)	2	Massachusetts	202-225-5601	202-225-8112	http://www.house.gov/writerep/
Rep. Jim McGovern (D)	3	Massachusetts	202-225-6101	202-225-5759	http://www.house.gov/writerep/
Rep. Barney Frank (D)	4	Massachusetts	202-225-5931	202-225-0182	http://www.house.gov/writerep/
Rep. Niki Tsongas (D)	5	Massachusetts	202-225-3411	202-226-0771	http://tsongas.house.gov/?sectionid=11&sectiontree=311
Rep. John Tierney (D)	6	Massachusetts	202-225-8020	202-225-5915	http://www.house.gov/tierney/IMA/email.shtml
Rep. Ed Markey (D)	7	Massachusetts	202-225-2836	202-226-0092	http://markey.house.gov/index.php?option=com_email_form&Itemid=124
Rep. Michael E. Capuano (D)	8	Massachusetts	202-225-5111	202-225-9322	http://www.house.gov/capuano/contact/email.shtml
Rep. Stephen F. Lynch (D)	9	Massachusetts	202-225-8273	202-225-3984	http://www.house.gov/writerep/
Rep. Bill Delahunt (D)	10	Massachusetts	202-225-3111	202-225-5658	william.delahunt@mail.house.gov

Member Name	District	State	DC Phone	DC FAX	Email
Rep. Bart Stupak (D)	1	Michigan	202-225-4735	202-225-4744	http://www.house.gov/stupak/IMA/issue2.htm
Rep. Pete Hoekstra (R)	2	Michigan	202-225-4401	202-226-0779	http://www.house.gov/formhoekstra/IMA/email.htm
Rep. Vern Ehlers (R)	3	Michigan	202-225-3831	202-225-5144	http://www.house.gov/writerep/
Rep. Dave Camp (R)	4	Michigan	202-225-3561	202-225-9679	http://camp.house.gov/Contact/
Rep. Dale E. Kildee (D)	5	Michigan	202-225-3611	202-225-6393	http://www.house.gov/kildee/contact_form.shtml
Rep. Fred Upton (R)	6	Michigan	202-225-3761	202-225-4986	http://www.house.gov/writerep/
Rep. Mark Schauer (D)	7	Michigan	202-225-6276	202-225-6281	http://schauer.house.gov/Contact/
Rep. Mike Rogers (R)	8	Michigan	202-225-4872	202-225-5820	http://www.mikerogers.house.gov/Contact.aspx
Rep. Gary Peters (D)	9	Michigan	202-225-5802	202-226-2356	https://forms.house.gov/peters/contact-form.shtml
Rep. Candice Miller (R)	10	Michigan	202-225-2106	202-226-1169	http://candicemiller.house.gov/Contact.aspx
Rep. Thaddeus McCotter (R)	11	Michigan	202-225-8171	202-225-2667	http://mccotter.house.gov/HoR/MI11/Contact/
Rep. Sandy Levin (D)	12	Michigan	202-225-4961	202-226-1033	http://www.house.gov/levin/levin_home_email.shtml
Rep. Carolyn Kilpatrick (D)	13	Michigan	202-225-2261	202-225-5730	http://www.house.gov/writerep/
Rep. John Conyers, Jr. (D)	14	Michigan	202-225-5126	202-225-0072	http://conyers.house.gov/index.cfm?FuseAction=Contact.OnlineContactForm
Rep. John D. Dingell (D)	15	Michigan	202-225-4071	202-226-0371	http://www.house.gov/writerep/
Rep. Tim Walz (D)	1	Minnesota	202-225-2472	202-225-3433	http://walz.house.gov/zip_auth.shtm
Rep. John Kline (R)	2	Minnesota	202-225-2271	202-225-2595	http://kline.house.gov/?sectionid=7&sectiontree=47
Rep. Erik Paulsen (R)	3	Minnesota	202-225-2871	202-225-6351	https://forms.house.gov/paulsen/contact-form.shtml
Rep. Betty McCollum (D)	4	Minnesota	202-225-6631	202-225-1968	http://forms.house.gov/mccollum/webforms/issue_subscribe.htm
Rep. Keith Ellison (D)	5	Minnesota	202-225-4755	202-225-4886	http://ellison.house.gov/index.php?option=com_content&task=view&id=87

Member Name	District	State	DC Phone	DC FAX	Email
Rep. Michele Bachmann (R)	6	Minnesota	202-225-2331	202-225-6475	http://bachmann.house.gov/Email/
Rep. Collin Peterson (D)	7	Minnesota	202-225-2165	202-225-1593	http://collinpeterson.house.gov/email.html
Rep. Jim Oberstar (D)	8	Minnesota	202-225-6211	202-225-0699	http://wwwc.house.gov/oberstar/zipauth.htm
Rep. Travis W. Childers (D)	1	Mississippi	202-225-4306	202-225-3549	https://forms.house.gov/childers/webforms/contact.htm
Rep. Bennie Thompson (D)	2	Mississippi	202-225-5876	202-225-5898	https://forms.house.gov/benniethompson/contact-form.shtml
Rep. Gregg Harper (R)	3	Mississippi	202-225-5031	202-225-5797	http://harper.house.gov/contact/
Rep. Gene Taylor (D)	4	Mississippi	202-225-5772	202-225-7074	https://forms.house.gov/genetaylor/webforms/zipauth.htm
Rep. William Lacy Clay, Jr. (D)	1	Missouri	202-225-2406	202-226-3717	http://lacyclay.house.gov/contact.shtml
Rep. Todd Akin (R)	2	Missouri	202-225-2561	202-225-2563	http://www.house.gov/akin/email.shtml
Rep. Russ Carnahan (D)	3	Missouri	202-225-2671	202-225-7452	https://forms.house.gov/carnahan/webforms/issue_subscribe.htm
Rep. Ike Skelton (D)	4	Missouri	202-225-2876	202-225-2695	http://www.house.gov/skelton/email.shtml
Rep. Emanuel Cleaver, II (D)	5	Missouri	202-225-4535	202-225-4403	http://www.house.gov/cleaver/IMA/issue.htm
Rep. Sam Graves (R)	6	Missouri	202-225-7041	202-225-8221	http://www.house.gov/graves/contact.shtml
Rep. Roy Blunt (R)	7	Missouri	202-225-6536	202-225-5604	http://www.blunt.house.gov/Contact.aspx
Rep. Jo Ann Emerson (R)	8	Missouri	202-225-4404	202-226-0326	http://www.house.gov/emerson/contact.shtml
Rep. Blaine Luetkemeyer (R)	9	Missouri	202-225-2956	202-225-5712	https://forms.house.gov/luetkemeyer/contact-form.shtml
Rep. Dennis Rehberg (R)	At Large	Montana	202-225-3211	202-225-5687	http://rehberg.house.gov/index.cfm?sectionid=62&sectiontree=662
Rep. Jeff Fortenberry (R)	1	Nebraska	202-225-4806	202-225-5686	http://fortenberry.house.gov/contactform_zipcheck.shtml
Rep. Lee Terry (R)	2	Nebraska	202-225-4155	202-226-5452	http://www.house.gov/formleeterry/IMA/issue.htm
Rep. Adrian Smith (R)	3	Nebraska	202-225-6435	202-225-0207	http://www.house.gov/formadriansmith/issues_subscribe.htm

Member Name	District	State	DC Phone	DC FAX	Email
Rep. Shelley Berkley (D)	1	Nevada	202-225-5965	202-225-3119	http://berkley.house.gov/contact/email.html
Rep. Dean Heller (R)	2	Nevada	202-225-6155	202-225-5679	http://www.house.gov/writerep/
Rep. Dina Titus (D)	3	Nevada	202-225-3252	202-225-2185	https://forms.house.gov/titus/contact-form.shtml
Rep. Carol Shea-Porter (D)	1	New Hampshire	202-225-5456	202-225-5822	http://forms.house.gov/shea-porter/webform/issue_subscribe.htm
Rep. Paul Hodes, II (D)	2	New Hampshire	202-225-5206	202-225-2946	http://hodes.house.gov/contact.aspx
Rep. Robert E. Andrews (D)	1	New Jersey	202-225-6501	202-225-6583	http://www.house.gov/andrews/contact_form_za.shtml
Rep. Frank A. LoBiondo (R)	2	New Jersey	202-225-6572	202-225-3318	http://www.house.gov/lobiondo/IMA/issue.htm
Rep. John Adler (D)	3	New Jersey	202-225-4765	202-225-0778	https://forms.house.gov/adler/contact-form.shtml
Rep. Chris H. Smith (R)	4	New Jersey	202-225-3765	202-225-7768	http://chrissmith.house.gov/zipauth.html
Rep. Scott Garrett (R)	5	New Jersey	202-225-4465	202-225-9048	http://garrett.house.gov/Contact/
Rep. Frank Pallone, Jr. (D)	6	New Jersey	202-225-4671	202-225-9665	http://www.house.gov/pallone/contact.shtml
Rep. Leonard Lance (R)	7	New Jersey	202-225-5361	202-225-9460	https://forms.house.gov/lance/contact-form.shtml
Rep. Bill Pascrell, Jr. (D)	8	New Jersey	202-225-5751	202-225-5782	http://pascrell.house.gov/contact/
Rep. Steve Rothman (D)	9	New Jersey	202-225-5061	202-225-5851	https://forms.house.gov/rothman/webforms/issue_subscribe.htm
Rep. Donald M. Payne (D)	10	New Jersey	202-225-3436	202-225-4160	http://www.house.gov/payne/IMA/email.shtml
Rep. Rodney Frelinghuysen (R)	11	New Jersey	202-225-5034	202-225-3186	http://frelinghuysen.house.gov/contactus/form.cfm
Rep. Rush Holt (D)	12	New Jersey	202-225-5801	202-225-6025	http://holt.house.gov/contact.shtml
Rep. Albio Sires (D)	13	New Jersey	202-225-7919	202-226-0792	https://forms.house.gov/sires/webforms/issue_subscribe.htm
Rep. Martin Heinrich (D)	1	New Mexico	202-225-6316	202-225-4975	https://forms.house.gov/heinrich/contact-form.shtml
Rep. Harry Teague (D)	2	New Mexico	202-225-2365	202-225-9599	http://forms.house.gov/teague/webforms/issue_subscribe.htm

Member Name	District	State	DC Phone	DC FAX	Email
Rep. Ben Ray Lujan (D)	3	New Mexico	202-225-6190	202-226-1528	https://forms.house.gov/lujan/contact-form.shtml
Rep. Tim Bishop (D)	1	New York	202-225-3826	202-225-3143	http://timbishop.house.gov/?sectionid=96&sectiontree=796
Rep. Steve Israel (D)	2	New York	202-225-3335	202-225-4669	http://www.house.gov/formisrael/contact.html
Rep. Pete King (R)	3	New York	202-225-7896	202-226-2279	Pete.King@mail.house.gov
Rep. Carolyn McCarthy (D)	4	New York	202-225-5516	202-225-5758	http://www.house.gov/writerep/
Rep. Gary Ackerman (D)	5	New York	202-225-2601	202-225-1589	http://www.house.gov/ackerman/pages/contact.html
Rep. Gregory W. Meeks (D)	6	New York	202-225-3461	202-226-4169	http://www.house.gov/meeks/contactform_zipcheck.shtml
Rep. Joseph Crowley (D)	7	New York	202-225-3965	202-225-1909	http://crowley.house.gov/contact.shtml
Rep. Jerrold Nadler (D)	8	New York	202-225-5635	202-225-6923	http://www.house.gov/nadler/emailform.shtml
Rep. Anthony Weiner (D)	9	New York	202-225-6616	202-226-7253	http://weiner.house.gov/email_anthony.aspx
Rep. Edolphus (Ed) Towns (D)	10	New York	202-225-5936	202-225-1018	http://www.house.gov/towns/contact_form.shtml
Rep. Yvette Clarke (D)	11	New York	202-225-6231	202-226-0112	http://clarke.house.gov/contactform_zipcheck.shtml
Rep. Nydia M. Velazquez (D)	12	New York	202-225-2361	202-226-0327	http://www.house.gov/velazquez/IMA/issue_subscribe.htm
Rep. Michael E. McMahon (D)	13	New York	202-225-3371	202-226-1272	https://forms.house.gov/mcmahon/contact-form.shtml
Rep. Carolyn B. Maloney (D)	14	New York	202-225-7944	202-225-4709	http://maloney.house.gov/index.php?option=com_email_form&Itemid=73
Rep. Charles B. Rangel (D)	15	New York	202-225-4365	202-225-0816	https://forms.house.gov/rangel/forms/contact.shtml
Rep. Jose E. Serrano (D)	16	New York	202-225-4361	202-225-6001	http://serrano.house.gov/Forms/Contact.aspx
Rep. Eliot L. Engel (D)	17	New York	202-225-2464	202-225-5513	http://www.house.gov/writerep/
Rep. Nita M. Lowey (D)	18	New York	202-225-6506	202-225-0546	http://lowey.house.gov/?sectionid=568&sectiontree=56
Rep. John J. Hall (D)	19	New York	202-225-5441	202-225-3289	http://johnhall.house.gov/emailjohn.asp

Member Name	District	State	DC Phone	DC FAX	Email
Rep. Scott Murphy (D)	20	New York	202-225-5614	202-225-1168	https://forms.house.gov/murphy/contact-form.shtml
Rep. Paul D. Tonko (D)	21	New York	202-225-5076	202-225-5077	https://forms.house.gov/tonko/contact-form.shtml
Rep. Maurice D. Hinchey (D)	22	New York	202-225-6335	202-226-0774	http://www.house.gov/hinchey/zipauth.shtml
Rep. John M. McHugh (R)	23	New York	202-225-4611	202-226-0621	http://mchugh.house.gov/zipauth.aspx
Rep. Michael A. Arcuri (D)	24	New York	202-225-3665	202-225-1891	http://arcuri.house.gov/IMA/issue_subscribe.htm
Rep. Dan Maffei (D)	25	New York	202-225-3701	202-225-4042	https://forms.house.gov/maffei/contact-form.shtml
Rep. Chris Lee (R)	26	New York	202-225-5265	202-225-5910	https://forms.house.gov/lee/contact-form.shtml
Rep. Brian Higgins (D)	27	New York	202-225-3306	202-226-0347	http://higgins.house.gov/email.shtml
Rep. Louise M. Slaughter (D)	28	New York	202-225-3615	202-225-7822	http://www.louise.house.gov/index.php?
Rep. G. K. Butterfield, Jr. (D)	1	North Carolina	202-225-3101	202-225-3354	http://butterfield.house.gov/contactinfo.asp
Rep. Bob Etheridge (D)	2	North Carolina	202-225-4531	202-225-5662	http://etheridge.house.gov/Contact/
Rep. Walter B. Jones, Jr. (R)	3	North Carolina	202-225-3415	202-225-3286	http://jones.house.gov/contact_form_email.cfm
Rep. David Price (D)	4	North Carolina	202-225-1784	202-225-2014	http://price.house.gov/contact/contact_form.shtml
Rep. Virginia Foxx (R)	5	North Carolina	202-225-2071	202-225-2995	http://www.house.gov/formfoxx/IMA/issue_subscribe.htm
Rep. Howard Coble (R)	6	North Carolina	202-225-3065	202-225-8611	howard.coble@mail.house.gov
Rep. Mike McIntyre (D)	7	North Carolina	202-225-2731	202-225-5773	http://www.house.gov/mcintyre/issue.shtml
Rep. Larry Kissell (D)	8	North Carolina	202-225-3715	202-225-4036	https://forms.house.gov/kissell/contact-form.shtml
Rep. Sue Myrick (R)	9	North Carolina	202-225-1976	202-225-3389	http://myrick.house.gov/zipauth.shtml
Rep. Patrick McHenry (R)	10	North Carolina	202-225-2576	202-225-0316	http://mchenry.house.gov/zipauth.htm

Member Name	District	State	DC Phone	DC FAX	Email
Rep. Heath Shuler (D)	11	North Carolina	202-225-6401	202-226-6422	http://shuler.house.gov/zipauth.htm
Rep. Mel Watt (D)	12	North Carolina	202-225-1510	202-225-1512	http://watt.house.gov/IQform.asp
Rep. Brad Miller (D)	13	North Carolina	202-225-3032	202-225-0181	http://bradmiller.house.gov/?sectionid=178&sectiontree=917
Rep. Earl Pomeroy (D)	At Large	North Dakota	202-225-2611	202-226-0893	http://www.house.gov/formpomeroy/zipauth.htm
Rep. Gregorio Camacho (Kilili) Sablan (I)	At Large	N. Mariana Islands	202-225-2646	202-226-4249	https://forms.house.gov/sablan/contact-form.shtml
Rep. Steve Driehaus (D)	1	Ohio	202-225-2216	202-225-3012	https://forms.house.gov/driehaus/webforms/issue_subscribe.htm
Rep. Jean Schmidt (R)	2	Ohio	202-225-3164	202-225-1992	http://www.house.gov/schmidt/contact.shtml
Rep. Michael Turner (R)	3	Ohio	202-225-6465	202-225-6754	http://turner.house.gov/Contact/
Rep. Jim Jordan (R)	4	Ohio	202-225-2676	202-226-0577	http://jordan.house.gov/contactform_zipcheck.shtml
Rep. Bob Latta (R)	5	Ohio	202-225-6405	202-225-1985	http://latta.house.gov/Contact/
Rep. Charlie Wilson (D)	6	Ohio	202-225-5705	202-225-5907	http://www.charliewilson.house.gov/index.php?
Rep. Steve Austria (R)	7	Ohio	202-225-4324	202-225-1984	https://forms.house.gov/austria/contact-form.shtml
Rep. John Boehner (R)	8	Ohio	202-225-6205	202-225-0704	http://johnboehner.house.gov/Contact/
Rep. Marcy Kaptur (D)	9	Ohio	202-225-4146	202-225-7711	http://www.kaptur.house.gov/index.php?
Rep. Dennis J. Kucinich (D)	10	Ohio	202-225-5871	202-225-5745	http://kucinich.house.gov/Contact/Starter.htm
Rep. Marcia L. Fudge (D)	11	Ohio	202-225-7032	202-225-1339	http://fudge.house.gov/?sectionid=51&sectiontree=351
Rep. Patrick J. Tiberi (R)	12	Ohio	202-225-5355	202-226-4523	http://www.house.gov/writerep/
Rep. Betty Sutton (D)	13	Ohio	202-225-3401	202-225-2266	http://sutton.house.gov/about/emailform.cfm
Rep. Steven C. LaTourette (R)	14	Ohio	202-225-5731	202-225-3307	http://latourette.house.gov/ContactSteve.aspx
Rep. Mary Jo Kilroy (D)	15	Ohio	202-225-2015	202-225-3529	https://forms.house.gov/kilroy/contact-form.shtml

Member Name	District	State	DC Phone	DC FAX	Email
Rep. John A. Boccieri (D)	16	Ohio	202-225-3876	202-225-3059	https://forms.house.gov/boccieri/contact-form.shtml
Rep. Tim Ryan (D)	17	Ohio	202-225-5261	202-225-3719	http://timryan.house.gov/index.php?option=com_content&
Rep. Zack Space (D)	18	Ohio	202-225-6265	202-225-3394	http://space.house.gov/?sectionid=61&sectiontree=2661
Rep. John Sullivan (R)	1	Oklahoma	202-225-2211	202-225-9187	http://sullivan.house.gov/zipauth.html
Rep. Dan Boren (D)	2	Oklahoma	202-225-2701	202-225-3038	http://www.house.gov/boren/emailsignup.shtml
Rep. Frank Lucas (R)	3	Oklahoma	202-225-5565	202-225-8698	https://forms.house.gov/lucas/contact-form.shtml
Rep. Tom Cole (R)	4	Oklahoma	202-225-6165	202-225-3512	http://www.cole.house.gov/contact-tom.html
Rep. Mary Fallin (R)	5	Oklahoma	202-225-2132	202-226-1463	http://fallin.house.gov/?sectionid=3&sectiontree=3
Rep. David Wu (D)	1	Oregon	202-225-0855	202-225-9497	http://www.house.gov/wu/email.shtml
Rep. Greg Walden (R)	2	Oregon	202-225-6730	202-225-5774	http://walden.house.gov/ContactGreg.Home.shtml
Rep. Earl Blumenauer (D)	3	Oregon	202-225-4811	202-225-8941	http://blumenauer.house.gov/index.php?option=com_email_form&Itemid=206
Rep. Peter DeFazio (D)	4	Oregon	202-225-6416	202-225-0032	http://www.house.gov/formdefazio/contact.html
Rep. Kurt Schrader (D)	5	Oregon	202-225-5711	202-225-5699	https://forms.house.gov/schrader/contact-form.shtml
Rep. Robert Brady (D)	1	Pennsylvania	202-225-4731	202-225-0088	http://www.house.gov/formrobertbrady/issue.htm
Rep. Chaka Fattah (D)	2	Pennsylvania	202-225-4001	202-225-5392	http://fattah.house.gov/?sectionid=88&sectiontree=8
Rep. Kathy Dahlkemper (D)	3	Pennsylvania2	02-225-5406	202-225-3103	https://forms.house.gov/dahlkemper/contact-form.shtml
Rep. Jason Altmire (D)	4	Pennsylvania	202-225-2565	202-226-2274	https://forms.house.gov/altmire/webforms/issue_subscribe.htm
Rep. Glenn (GT) Thompson (R)	5	Pennsylvania	202-225-5121	202-225-5796	https://forms.house.gov/thompson/contact-form.shtml
Rep. Jim Gerlach (R)	6	Pennsylvania	202-225-4315	202-225-8440	http://www.house.gov/writerep/
Rep. Joe Sestak (D)	7	Pennsylvania	202-225-2011	202-226-0280	http://sestak.house.gov/IMA/issue_subscribe.htm

Member Name	District	State	DC Phone	DC FAX	Email
Rep. Patrick J. Murphy (D)	8	Pennsylvania	202-225-4276	202-225-9511	http://www.patrickmurphy.house.gov/index.php?
Rep. Bill Shuster (R)	9	Pennsylvania	202-225-2431	202-225-2486	http://www.house.gov/shuster/zipauth.htm
Rep. Christopher P. Carney (D	10	Pennsylvania	202-225-3731	202-225-9594	http://carney.house.gov/contact.shtml
Rep. Paul E. Kanjorski (D) 1	1	Pennsylvania	202-225-6511	202-225-0764	http://kanjorski.house.gov/index.php?
Rep. Allyson Y. Schwartz (D)	13	Pennsylvania	202-225-6111	202-226-0611	http://schwartz.house.gov/issue_subscribe.shtml
Rep. Mike Doyle (D)	14	Pennsylvania	202-225-2135	202-225-3084	http://doyle.house.gov/email_mike.shtml
Rep. Charlie Dent (R)	15	Pennsylvania	202-225-6411	202-226-0778	http://dent.house.gov/contact.aspx
Rep. Joe Pitts (R)	16	Pennsylvania	202-225-2411	202-225-2013	http://www.house.gov/pitts/contact.shtml
Rep. Tim Holden (D)	17	Pennsylvania	02-225-5546	202-226-0996	http://holden.house.gov/contactform_zipcheck.shtml
Rep. Tim Murphy (R)	18	Pennsylvania	202-225-2301	202-225-1844	http://murphy.house.gov/?sectionid=7&sectiontree=47
Rep. Todd Russell Platts (R)	19	Pennsylvania	202-225-5836	202-226-1000	http://www.house.gov/platts/email.shtml
Resident Cmmr. Pedro Pierluisi (D)	At Large	Puerto Rico	202-225-2615	202-225-2154	https://forms.house.gov/pierluisi/contact-form.shtml
Rep. Patrick J. Kennedy (D)	1	Rhode Island	202-225-4911	202-225-3290	http://www.house.gov/formpatrickkennedy/IMA/issue.htm
Rep. Jim Langevin (D)	2	Rhode Island	202-225-2735	202-225-5976	http://langevin.house.gov/comments.shtml
Rep. Henry E. Brown, Jr. (R)	1	South Carolina	202-225-3176	202-225-3407	http://brown.house.gov/Contact/writebrown.html
Rep. Joe Wilson (R)	2	South Carolina	202-225-2452	202-225-2455	http://www.house.gov/formwilson/IMA/issue.htm
Rep. J. Gresham Barrett (R)	3	South Carolina	202-225-5301	202-225-3216	http://www.house.gov/formbarrett/writebarrett.htm
Rep. Bob Inglis (R)	4	South Carolina	202-225-6030	202-226-1177	http://inglis.house.gov/contact.asp?
Rep. John Spratt (D)	5	South Carolina	202-225-5501	202-225-0464	http://www.house.gov/spratt/email_john.shtml

Member Name	District	State	DC Phone	DC FAX	Email
Rep. James E. Clyburn (D)	6	South Carolina	202-225-3315	202-225-2313	http://clyburn.house.gov/zip_code_verify.cfm
Rep. Stephanie Herseth Sandlin (D)	At Large	South Dakota	202-225-2801	202-225-5823	http://hersethsandlin.house.gov/contact2.htm
Rep. Phil Roe (R)	1	Tennessee	202-225-6356	202-225-5714	https://forms.house.gov/roe/contact-form.shtml
Rep. John J. Duncan, Jr. (R)	2	Tennessee	202-225-5435	202-225-6440	http://www.house.gov/duncan/contactform_zipcheck.shtml
Rep. Zach Wamp (R)	3	Tennessee	202-225-3271	202-225-3494	http://www.house.gov/wamp/contact_email.shtm
Rep. Lincoln Davis (D)	4	Tennessee	202-225-6831	202-226-5172	http://www.house.gov/writerep/
Rep. Jim Cooper (D)	5	Tennessee	202-225-4311	202-226-1035	http://www.cooper.house.gov/index.php?
Rep. Bart Gordon (D)	6	Tennessee	202-225-4231	202-225-6887	http://gordon.house.gov/contact/contact_form.shtml
Rep. Marsha Blackburn (R)	7	Tennessee	202-225-2811	202-225-3004	http://blackburn.house.gov/contactform/
Rep. John Tanner (D)	8	Tennessee	202-225-4714	202-225-1765	http://www.house.gov/writerep/
Rep. Steve Cohen (D)	9	Tennessee	202-225-3265	202-225-5663	http://cohen.house.gov/index.php?option=com_email_form&Itemid=111
Rep. Louie Gohmert (R)	1	Texas	202-225-3035	202-226-1230	http://gohmert.house.gov/?sectionid=36&sectiontree=36
Rep. Ted Poe (R)	2	Texas	202-225-6565	202-225-5547	http://poe.house.gov/contact/contactform.htm
Rep. Sam Johnson (R)	3	Texas2	02-225-4201	202-225-1485	http://www.house.gov/formsamjohnson/IMA/issue.htm
Rep. Ralph Hall (R)	4	Texas	202-225-6673	202-225-3332	http://www.house.gov/ralphhall/IMA/zipauth.htm
Rep. Jeb Hensarling (R)	5	Texas	202-225-3484	202-226-4888	http://www.house.gov/hensarling/contact_web.shtml
Rep. Joe Barton (R)	6	Texas	202-225-2002	202-225-3052	http://joebarton.house.gov/ContactJoe.aspx?Type=Contact
Rep. John Culberson (R)	7	Texas	202-225-2571	202-225-4381	http://www.culberson.house.gov/contactinfo.aspx
Rep. Kevin Brady (R)	8	Texas	202-225-4901	202-225-5524	rep.brady@mail.house.gov
Rep. Al Green (D)	9	Texas	202-225-7508	202-225-2947	http://www.house.gov/writerep/

Member Name	District	State	DC Phone	DC FAX	Email
Rep. Michael T. McCaul (R)	10	Texas	202-225-2401	202-225-5955	http://mccaul.house.gov/?sectionid=78&sectiontree=378
Rep. Mike Conaway (R)	11	Texas	202-225-3605	202-225-1783	http://conaway.house.gov/contact/
Rep. Kay Granger (R)	12	Texas	202-225-5071	202-225-5683	http://kaygranger.house.gov/?sectionid=46&sectiontree=46
Rep. Mac Thornberry (R)	13	Texas	202-225-3706	202-225-3486	http://www.house.gov/writerep/
Rep. Ron Paul (R)	14	Texas	202-225-2831	202-228-2862	http://www.house.gov/paul/contact.shtml
Rep. Ruben Hinojosa (D)	15	Texas	202-225-2531	202-225-5688	http://www.house.gov/writerep/
Rep. Silvestre Reyes (D)	16	Texas	202-225-4831	202-225-2016	http://reyes.house.gov/Contact/vyo.htm
Rep. Chet Edwards (D)	17	Texas	202-225-6105	202-225-0350	https://forms.house.gov/edwards/webforms/issue_subscribe.htm
Rep. Sheila Jackson-Lee (D)	18	Texas	202-225-3816	202-225-3317	http://www.jacksonlee.house.gov/contact.shtml
Rep. Randy Neugebauer (R)	19	Texas	202-225-4005	202-225-9615	http://www.randy.house.gov/?sectionid=65&sectiontree=865
Rep. Charles A. Gonzalez (D)	20	Texas	202-225-3236	202-225-1915	http://www.gonzalez.house.gov/index.php?
Rep. Lamar Smith (R)	21	Texas	202-225-4236	202-225-8628	http://lamarsmith.house.gov/contact.aspx?section=Mail
Rep. Pete Olson (R)	22	Texas	202-225-5951	202-225-5241	https://forms.house.gov/olson/contact-form.shtml
Rep. Ciro Rodriguez (D)	23	Texas	202-225-4511	202-225-2237	http://www.rodriguez.house.gov/index.php?
Rep. Kenny Marchant (R)	24	Texas	202-225-6605	202-225-0074	http://marchant.house.gov/emailkenny.shtml
Rep. Lloyd Doggett (D)	25	Texas	202-225-4865	202-225-3073	http://forms.house.gov/doggett/webforms/issue_subscribe.htm
Rep. Michael Burgess (R)	26	Texas	202-225-7772	202-225-2919	http://burgess.house.gov/Contact/Offices/
Rep. Solomon P. Ortiz (D)	27	Texas	202-225-7742	202-226-1134	http://www.house.gov/formortiz/issue.htm
Rep. Henry Cuellar (D)	28	Texas	202-225-1640	202-225-1641	http://cuellar.house.gov/Contact/SendMeAnEmail.htm
Rep. Gene Green (D)	29	Texas	202-225-1688	202-225-9903	http://www.house.gov/green/contact/

Member Name	District	State	DC Phone	DC FAX	Email
Rep. Eddie Bernice Johnson (D)	30	Texas	202-225-8885	202-226-1477	http://ebjohnson.house.gov/?sectionid=3&sectiontree=3
Rep. John Carter (R)	31	Texas	202-225-3864	202-225-5886	http://www.house.gov/writerep/
Rep. Pete Sessions (R)	32	Texas	202-225-2231	202-225-5878	http://sessions.house.gov/index.cfm?FuseAction=ContactUs.ContactForm
Rep. Rob Bishop (R)	1	Utah	202-225-0453	202-225-5857	http://robbishop.house.gov/ZipAuth.aspx
Rep. James D. Matheson (D)	2	Utah	202-225-3011	202-225-5638	https://forms.house.gov/matheson/contact.shtml
Rep. Jason Chaffetz (R)	3	Utah	202-225-7751	202-225-5629	https://forms.house.gov/chaffetz/contact-form.shtml
Rep. Peter Welch (D)	At Large	Vermont	202-225-4115	202-225-6790	http://www.house.gov/formwelch/issue_subscribe.htm
Del. Donna M. Christensen (D)	At Large	Virgin Islands	202-225-1790	202-225-5517	http://www.house.gov/writerep/
Rep. Robert J. Wittman (R)	1	Virginia	202-225-4261	202-225-4382	https://forms.house.gov/wittman/IMA/webforms/issue_subscribe.htm
Rep. Glenn Nye, III (D)	2	Virginia	202-225-4215	202-225-4218	https://forms.house.gov/nye/contact-form.shtml
Rep. Robert C. Scott (D)	3	Virginia	202-225-8351	202-225-8354	http://www.house.gov/writerep/
Rep. J. Randy Forbes (R)	4	Virginia	202-225-6365	202-226-1170	http://randyforbes.house.gov/Contact/ZipAuth.htm
Rep. Tom Perriello (D)	5	Virginia	202-225-4711	202-225-5681	https://forms.house.gov/perriello/contact-form.shtml
Rep. Bob Goodlatte (R)	6	Virginia	202-225-5431	202-225-9681	http://www.house.gov/goodlatte/emailbob.htm
Rep. Eric I. Cantor (R)	7	Virginia	202-225-2815	202-225-0011	http://www.house.gov/writerep/
Rep. James P. Moran (D)	8	Virginia	202-225-4376	202-225-0017	http://moran.house.gov/zipauth.shtml
Rep. Rick Boucher (D)	9	Virginia	202-225-3861	202-225-0442	http://www.boucher.house.gov/index.php?
Rep. Frank R. Wolf (R)	10	Virginia	202-225-5136	202-225-0437	http://www.house.gov/formwolf/contact_email/emailzip.shtml
Rep. Gerry Connolly (D)	11	Virginia	202-225-1492	202-225-3071	http://gerryconnolly.house.gov/?sectionid=50&sectiontree=350
Rep. Jay Inslee (D)	1	Washington	202-225-6311	202-226-1606	http://www.house.gov/inslee/contact/email.html

Member Name	District	State	DC Phone	DC FAX	Email
Rep. Rick R. Larsen (D)	2	Washington	202-225-2605 2	02-225-4420	http://www.house.gov/larsen/IMA/issue_subscribe.shtml
Rep. Brian Baird (D)	3	Washington	202-225-3536	202-225-3478	https://forms.house.gov/baird/webforms/issue_subscribe.htm
Rep. Richard (Doc) Hastings (R)	4	Washington	202-225-5816	202-225-3251	http://hastings.house.gov/ContactForm.aspx
Rep. Cathy McMorris Rodgers (R)	5	Washington	202-225-2006	202-225-3392	http://mcmorris.house.gov/?sectionid=82&sectiontree=482
Rep. Norman D. Dicks (D)	6	Washington	202-225-5916	202-226-1176	http://www.house.gov/dicks/email.shtml
Rep. Jim McDermott (D)	7	Washington	202-225-3106	202-225-6197	http://www.house.gov/mcdermott/contact.shtml
Rep. Dave Reichert (R)	8	Washington	202-225-7761	202-225-4282	http://reichert.house.gov/Contact/ZipAuth.htm
Rep. Adam Smith (D)	9	Washington	202-225-8901	202-225-5893	http://adamsmith.house.gov/Contact/
Rep. Alan B. Mollohan (D)	1	West Virginia	202-225-4172	202-225-7564	CongressmanMollohan@mail.house.gov
Rep. Shelley Moore Capito (R)	2	West Virginia	202-225-2711	202-225-7856	http://www.house.gov/writerep/
Rep. Nick Joe Rahall, II (D)	3	West Virginia	202-225-3452	202-225-9061	http://www.rahall.house.gov/?sectionid=9&sectiontree=9
Rep. Paul Ryan (R)	1	Wisconsin	202-225-3031	202-225-3393	http://www.house.gov/ryan/email.htm
Rep. Tammy Baldwin (D)	2	Wisconsin	202-225-2906	202-225-6942	http://tammybaldwin.house.gov/get_address.html
Rep. Ron Kind (D)	3	Wisconsin	202-225-5506	202-225-5739	http://www.kind.house.gov/?sectionid=18&sectiontree=18
Rep. Gwen Moore (D)	4	Wisconsin	202-225-4572	202-225-8135	http://www.house.gov/gwenmoore/contact.shtml
Rep. F. James Sensenbrenner, Jr. (R)	5	Wisconsin	202-225-5101	202-225-3190	http://sensenbrenner.house.gov/email_zip.htm
Rep. Thomas E. Petri (R)	6	Wisconsin	202-225-2476	202-225-2356	https://forms.house.gov/petri/zip_authen.shtml
Rep. David R. Obey (D)	7	Wisconsin	202-225-3365	202-225-3240	http://www.obey.house.gov/index.php?
Rep. Steve Kagen (D)	8	Wisconsin	202-225-5665	202-225-5729	https://forms.house.gov/kagen/webforms/contact.shtml
Rep. Cynthia Lummis (R)	At Large	Wyoming	202-225-2311	202-225-3057	https://forms.house.gov/lummis/contact-form.shtml

★ SENATE MEMBERS ★

Member Name	State	DC Phone	DC FAX	Email
Jeff Sessions (R)	Alabama	202-224-4124	202-224-3149	http://sessions.senate.gov/public/index.cfm?
Sen. Richard C. Shelby (R)	Alabama	202-224-5744	202-224-3416	http://shelby.senate.gov/public/index.cfm?
Sen. Lisa Murkowski (R)	Alaska	202-224-6665	202-224-5301	http://murkowski.senate.gov/public/index.cfm?
Sen. Mark Begich (D)	Alaska	202-224-3004	202-224-2354	http://begich.senate.gov/contact/contact.cfm
Sen. John McCain (R)	Arizona	202-224-2235	202-228-2862	http://mccain.senate.gov/public/index.cfm?
Sen. Jon Kyl (R)	Arizona2	02-224-4521	202-224-2207	http://kyl.senate.gov/contact.cfm
Sen. Blanche Lambert Lincoln (D)	Arkansas	202-224-4843	202-228-1371	http://lincoln.senate.gov/contact/email.cfm
Sen. Mark Pryor (D)	Arkansas	202-224-2353	202-228-0908	http://pryor.senate.gov/contact/
Sen. Barbara Boxer (D)	California	202-224-3553	202-224-0454	http://boxer.senate.gov/contact/email/policy.cfm
Sen. Dianne Feinstein (D)	California	202-224-3841	202-228-3954	http://feinstein.senate.gov/public/index.cfm?
Sen. Mark Udall (D)	Colorado	202-224-5941	202-224-6471	http://markudall.senate.gov/contact/contact.cfm
Sen. Michael F. Bennet (D)	Colorado	202-224-5852	202-228-5036	http://bennet.senate.gov/public/?p=TransitionalSiteEmailSenatorBennet
Sen. Christopher J. Dodd (D)	Connecticut	202-224-2823	202-224-1083	http://dodd.senate.gov/index.php?q=node/3128&cat=Opinion
Sen. Joseph I. Lieberman (ID)	Connecticut	202-224-4041	202-224-9750	http://lieberman.senate.gov/contact/index.cfm?regarding=issue
Sen. Ted Kaufman (D)	Delaware	202-224-5042	202-228-3075	http://kaufman.senate.gov/services/contact/
Sen. Thomas R. Carper (D)	Delaware	202-224-2441	202-228-2190	http://carper.senate.gov/contact/
Sen. Bill Nelson (D)	Florida	202-224-5274	202-228-2183	http://billnelson.senate.gov/contact/email.cfm
Sen. Mel Martinez (R)	Florida	202-224-3041	202-228-5171	http://martinez.senate.gov/public/?p=EmailSenatorMartinez
Sen. Johnny Isakson (R)	Georgia	202-224-3643	202-228-0724	http://isakson.senate.gov/contact.cfm

Member Name	State	DC Phone	DC FAX	Email
Sen. Saxby Chambliss (R)	Georgia	202-224-3521	202-224-0103	http://chambliss.senate.gov/public/index.cfm?
Sen. Dan Inouye (D)	Hawaii	202-224-3934	202-224-6747	http://inouye.senate.gov/Contact/Email-Form.cfm
Sen. Daniel K. Akaka (D)	Hawaii	202-224-6361	202-224-2126	http://akaka.senate.gov/public/index.cfm?FuseAction=Contact.Home
Sen. Jim Risch (R)	Idaho	02-224-2752	202-224-2573	http://risch.senate.gov/public/index.cfm?p=Email
Sen. Mike Crapo (R)	Idaho	202-224-6142	202-228-1375	http://crapo.senate.gov/contact/email.cfm
Sen. Richard J. Durbin (D)	Illinois	202-224-2152	202-228-0400	http://durbin.senate.gov/contact.cfm
Sen. Roland Burris (D)	Illinois	202-224-2854	202-228-3333	http://burris.senate.gov/contact/contact.cfm
Sen. Evan Bayh (D)	Indiana	202-224-5623	202-228-1377	http://bayh.senate.gov/contact/email/
Sen. Richard G. Lugar (R)	Indiana	202-224-4814	202-228-0360	http://lugar.senate.gov/contact/
Sen. Charles E. Grassley (R)	Iowa	202-224-3744	202-224-6020	http://grassley.senate.gov/contact.cfm
Sen. Tom Harkin (D)	Iowa	202-224-3254	202-224-9369	https://harkin.senate.gov/c/index.cfm
Sen. Pat Roberts (R)	Kansas	202-224-4774	202-224-3514	http://roberts.senate.gov/public/index.cfm?
Sen. Sam Brownback (R)	Kansas	202-224-6521	202-228-1265	http://brownback.senate.gov/public/contact/emailsam.cfm
Sen. Jim Bunning (R)	Kentucky	202-224-4343	202-228-1373	http://bunning.senate.gov/public/index.cfm?
Sen. Mitch McConnell (R)	Kentucky	202-224-2541	202-224-2499	http://mcconnell.senate.gov/contact_form.cfm
Sen. David Vitter (R)	Louisiana	202-224-4623	202-228-5061	http://vitter.senate.gov/public/index.cfm?
Sen. Mary Landrieu (D)	Louisiana	202-224-5824	202-224-9735	http://landrieu.senate.gov/contact/index.cfm
Sen. Olympia Snowe (R)	Maine	202-224-5344	202-224-1946	http://snowe.senate.gov/public/index.cfm?
Sen. Susan Collins (R)	Maine	202-224-2523	202-224-2693	http://collins.senate.gov/public/continue.cfm?
Sen. Barbara A. Mikulski (D)	Maryland	202-224-4654	202-224-8858	http://mikulski.senate.gov/Contact/contact.cfm

Member Name	State	DC Phone	DC FAX	Email
Sen. Benjamin L. Cardin (D)	Maryland	202-224-4524	202-224-1651	http://cardin.senate.gov/contact/email.cfm
Sen. Scott P. Brown (R)	Massachusetts	202-224-4543	202-224-2417	http://Scott.P.Brown@state.ma.us
Sen. John F. Kerry (D)	Massachusetts	202-224-2742	202-224-8525	http://kerry.senate.gov/contact/email.cfm
Sen. Carl Levin (D)	Michigan	202-224-6221	202-224-1388	http://levin.senate.gov/contact/
Sen. Debbie A. Stabenow (D)	Michigan	202-224-4822	202-228-0325	http://stabenow.senate.gov/email.cfm
Sen. Amy Klobuchar (D)	Minnesota	202-224-3244	202-228-2186	http://klobuchar.senate.gov/emailamy.cfm
Sen. Roger F. Wicker (R)	Mississippi	202-224-6253	202-228-0378	http://wicker.senate.gov/public/index.cfm?
Sen. Thad Cochran (R)	Mississippi	202-224-5054	202-224-9450	http://cochran.senate.gov/email.html
Sen. Claire McCaskill (D)	Missouri	202-224-6154	202-228-6326	http://mccaskill.senate.gov/contact/
Sen. Kit Bond (R)	Missouri	202-224-5721	202-224-8149	http://bond.senate.gov/public/index.cfm?
Sen. Jon Tester (D)	Montana	202-224-2644	202-224-8594	http://tester.senate.gov/Contact/index.cfm
Sen. Max Baucus (D)	Montana	202-224-2651	202-224-9412	http://baucus.senate.gov/contact/emailForm.cfm?subj=issue
Sen. Ben Nelson (D)	Nebraska	202-224-6551	202-228-0012	http://bennelson.senate.gov/contact-me.cfm
Sen. Mike Johanns (R)	Nebraska	202-224-4224	202-228-0436	http://johanns.senate.gov/public/?p=EmailSenatorJohanns
Sen. Harry Reid (D)	Nevada	202-224-3542	202-224-7327	http://reid.senate.gov/contact/index.cfm
Sen. John Ensign (R)	Nevada	202-224-6244	202-228-2193	http://ensign.senate.gov/public/index.cfm?
Sen. Jeanne Shaheen (D)	New Hampshire	202-224-2841	202-228-3194	http://shaheen.senate.gov/contact/
Sen. Judd Gregg (R)	New Hampshire	202-224-3324	202-224-4952	http://gregg.senate.gov/public/index.cfm?
Sen. Frank Lautenberg (D)	New Jersey	202-224-3224	202-228-4054	http://lautenberg.senate.gov/contact/index1.cfm
Sen. Robert Menendez (D)	New Jersey	202-224-4744	202-228-2197	http://menendez.senate.gov/contact/contact.cfm

Member Name	State	DC Phone	DC FAX	Email
Sen. Jeff Bingaman (D)	New Mexico	202-224-5521	202-224-2852	http://bingaman.senate.gov/contact/types/email-issue.cfm
Sen. Tom Udall (D)	New Mexico	202-224-6621	202-228-3261	http://tomudall.senate.gov/contact/contact.cfm
Sen. Charles Schumer (D)	New York	202-224-6542	202-228-3027	http://schumer.senate.gov/new_website/contact.cfm
Sen. Kirsten Gillibrand (D)	New York	202-224-4451	202-228-0282	http://gillibrand.senate.gov/contact/
Sen. Kay Hagan (D)	North Carolina	202-224-6342	202-228-2563	http://hagan.senate.gov/?p=contact
Sen. Richard Burr (R)	North Carolina	202-224-3154	202-228-2981	http://burr.senate.gov/public/index.cfm?FuseAction=Contact.ContactForm
Sen. Byron L. Dorgan (D)	North Dakota	202-224-2551	202-224-1193	http://dorgan.senate.gov/contact/contact_form.cfm
Sen. Kent Conrad (D)	North Dakota	202-224-2043	202-224-7776	https://conrad.senate.gov/contact/webform.cfm
Sen. George Voinovich (R)	Ohio	202-224-3353	202-228-1382	http://voinovich.senate.gov/public/index.cfm?
Sen. Sherrod Brown (D)	Ohio	202-224-2315	202-228-6321	http://brown.senate.gov/contact/
Sen. James M. Inhofe (R)	Oklahoma	202-224-4721	202-228-0380	http://www.inhofe.senate.gov/public/
Sen. Tom Coburn (R)	Oklahoma	202-224-5754	202-224-6008	http://coburn.senate.gov/public/index.cfm?
Sen. Jeff Merkley (D)	Oregon	202-224-3753	202-228-3997	http://merkley.senate.gov/contact/
Sen. Ron Wyden (D)	Oregon	202-224-5244	202-228-2717	http://wyden.senate.gov/contact/
Sen. Arlen Specter (D)	Pennsylvania	202-224-4254	202-228-1229	http://specter.senate.gov/public/index.cfm?
Sen. Robert P. Casey (D)	Pennsylvania	202-224-6324	202-228-0604	http://casey.senate.gov/contact/
Sen. Jack Reed (D)	Rhode Island	202-224-4642	202-224-4680	http://reed.senate.gov/contact/contact-share.cfm
Sen. Sheldon Whitehouse (D)	Rhode Island	202-224-2921	202-228-6362	http://whitehouse.senate.gov/contact/
Sen. James DeMint (R)	South Carolina	202-224-6121	202-228-5143	http://demint.senate.gov/public/index.cfm?FuseAction=Contact.Home
Sen. Lindsey Graham (R)	South Carolina	202-224-5972 2	02-224-3808	http://lgraham.senate.gov/public/index.cfm?

Member Name	State	DC Phone	DC FAX	Email
Sen. John R. Thune (R)	South Dakota	202-224-2321	202-228-5429	http://thune.senate.gov/public/index.cfm?FuseAction=Contact.Email
Sen. Tim Johnson (D)	South Dakota	202-224-5842	202-228-5765	http://johnson.senate.gov/contact/
Sen. Bob Corker (R)	Tennessee	202-224-3344	202-228-0566	http://corker.senate.gov/public/index.cfm?
Sen. Lamar Alexander (R)	Tennessee	202-224-4944	202-228-3398	http://alexander.senate.gov/public/index.cfm?FuseAction=Contact.Home
Sen. John Cornyn (R)	Texas	202-224-2934	202-228-2856	http://cornyn.senate.gov/public/index.cfm?
Sen. Kay Bailey Hutchison (R)	Texas	202-224-5922	202-224-0776	http://hutchison.senate.gov/contact.cfm
Sen. Orrin G. Hatch (R)	Utah	202-224-5251	202-224-6331	http://hatch.senate.gov/public/index.cfm?FuseAction=Offices.Contact
Sen. Robert F. Bennett (R)	Utah	202-224-5444	202-228-1168	http://bennett.senate.gov/public/index.cfm?p=ContactForm
Sen. Bernie Sanders (I)	Vermont	202-224-5141	202-228-0776	http://www.sanders.senate.gov/comments/
Sen. Patrick J. Leahy (D)	Vermont	202-224-4242	202-224-3479	senator_leahy@leahy.senate.gov
Sen. James Webb (D)	Virginia	202-224-4024	202-228-6363	http://webb.senate.gov/contact/
Sen. Mark Warner (D)	Virginia	202-224-2023	202-224-6295	http://warner.senate.gov/public/index.cfm?p=Contact
Sen. Maria Cantwell (D)	Washington	202-224-3441	202-228-0514	http://cantwell.senate.gov/contact/index.cfm
Sen. Patty Murray (D)	Washington	202-224-2621	202-224-0238	http://murray.senate.gov/email/index.cfm
Sen. John D. (Jay) Rockefeller, IV (D)	West Virginia	202-224-6472	202-224-7665	http://rockefeller.senate.gov/contact/email.cfm
Sen. Robert C. Byrd (D)	West Virginia	202-224-3954	202-228-0002	http://byrd.senate.gov//contacts/index.cfm?ID=54
Sen. Herb Kohl (D)	Wisconsin	202-224-5653	202-224-9787	http://kohl.senate.gov/contact.cfm
Sen. Russell D. Feingold (D)	Wisconsin	202-224-5323	202-224-2725	http://feingold.senate.gov/contact_opinion.html
Sen. John A. Barrasso (R)	Wyoming	202-224-6441	202-224-1724	http://barrasso.senate.gov/public/index.cfm?
Sen. Michael Enzi (R)	Wyoming	202-224-3424	202-228-0359	http://enzi.senate.gov/public/index.cfm?

NOTES

NOTES

NOTES

NOTES

NOTES

NOTES

NOTES

NOTES

NOTES

NOTES

NOTES

Ic- 9/10 **WITHDRAWN**